The Power *of*
Purpose

er

Coauthor of the bestselling *Repacking Your Bags*

The Power *of* Purpose

Find Meaning,
Live Longer, Better

THIRD EDITION
Revised & Expanded

BK

Berrett–Koehler Publishers, Inc.
a BK Life book

Berrett-Koehler Publishers, Inc.
1333 Broadway, Suite 1000
Oakland, CA 94612-1921
Tel: (510) 817-2277   Fax: (510) 817-2278   www.bkconnection.com

Ordering Information

Quantity sales. Special discounts are available on quantity purchases by corporations, associations, and others. For details, contact the "Special Sales Department" at the Berrett-Koehler address above.

Individual sales. Berrett-Koehler publications are available through most bookstores. They can also be ordered directly from Berrett-Koehler: Tel: (800) 929-2929; Fax: (802) 864-7626; www.bkconnection.com

Orders for college textbook/course adoption use. Please contact Berrett-Koehler: Tel: (800) 929-2929; Fax: (802) 864-7626.

Orders by U.S. trade bookstores and wholesalers. Please contact Ingram Publisher Services, Tel: (800) 509-4887; Fax: (800) 838-1149; E-mail: customer.service@ingrampublisherservices.com; or visit www.ingrampublisherservices.com/Ordering for details about electronic ordering.

Berrett-Koehler and the BK logo are registered trademarks of Berrett-Koehler Publishers, Inc.

Printed in the United States of America

Berrett-Koehler books are printed on long-lasting acid-free paper. When it is available, we choose paper that has been manufactured by environmentally responsible processes. These may include using trees grown in sustainable forests, incorporating recycled paper, minimizing chlorine in bleaching, or recycling the energy produced at the paper mill.

Library of Congress Cataloging-in-Publication Data
Leider, Richard.
The power of purpose : find meaning, live longer, better / Richard Leider, Coauthor of the bestselling Life Reimagined. — Third Edition, Revised and Expanded.
    pages cm
Revised edition of the author's The power of purpose, 2010.
Includes bibliographical references and index.
ISBN 978-1-62656-636-1 (pbk. : alk. paper)
1. Conduct of life. 2. Vocation. 3. Self-realization. I. Title.
BF637.C5L44 2015
158--dc23
                                        2015021227

Third Edition
20 19 18 17 16 15   10 9 8 7 6 5 4 3 2 1

Cover: Irene Morris Design
Text design: Detta Penna
Copyedit: Kathleen Rake
Index: Dianna Haught

Contents

〜

Why Do You Get Up
in the Morning?

Your purpose.
Your aim or direction.
Your reason for being.
Your reason for getting up in the morning.

You may not have considered the first three items, but most of us have wondered about a reason to get up in the morning, at least occasionally. *The Power of Purpose, Third Edition,* is about that reason: to help you unlock the power of purpose in your life.

What Is Purpose?

Our purpose is the essence of who we are and what makes us unique.

Our purpose is an active expression of the deepest dimension within us—where we have a profound sense of who we are and why we're here.

Purpose is the aim around which we structure our lives, a source of direction and energy. Through the lens of purpose, we are able to see ourselves—and our future—more clearly.

You have a purpose no matter what age you are,

how healthy you are, or what your economic or social situation is. Your purpose is the reason you were born, and it can be what gets you out of bed in the morning.

Purpose is actively living your values, leaning toward compassion for others, and getting up in the morning to contribute value to the world.

Purpose is what gives life a meaning.

What Is the Power in Purpose?

Power is the other key word in the book's title that needs attention. Webster's Dictionary defines power as the "ability to do, act, or produce." Only certain kinds of purpose have the potential to be empowering, so being deliberate about identifying our purpose is essential. What determines the power in purpose, ultimately, is the worthiness of the aim. Having purpose that provides real power requires an aim outside ourselves. Only when our purpose is larger than ourselves can meaning be deeply savored and long lasting, not just a goal completed and then forgotten.

At our very core we need to matter. We need evidence to believe that we are growing and are giving—becoming the best we can be. Naming our purpose helps us satisfy a basic need that we're being used for a purpose that we recognize as worthy.

Many of us say we don't have enough time to take care of our careers and our lives. Then before we know it, we're right! We are so busy trying to survive in an increasingly complex world that we don't have time to notice time passing. We do many things to answer the question Why do I get up in the morning? However, our busyness can also be a way of avoiding the question. In addition, it is an anxious way of living that can lead to unease and psychological and physical problems. And finally, we might end up asking, What have I done with my life?

How Do You Unlock It?

There is a better way. Having a reason to get up in the morning can add not only years to your life, but also life to your years!

Finding that reason is not easy. If it were, we'd all know exactly why we're here and be living that purpose every minute of every day. However, my experience shows that when you unlock a clear sense of who you are, everything else follows naturally.

Some people will come to the purpose quest with a natural bent toward reflection. Others will find the process uncomfortable, or unnatural. A few will just roll their eyes. The key to engaging both the seekers and the skeptics is to offer a step-by-step practical guidance process. And, that's what this book offers to you.

If you are looking for a reason to get up in the morning or asking questions such as these, this book is for you:

- I feel that I've missed my calling in life. How do I find it?

- I've successfully reached midlife. Is that all there is? What's next?

- I've been growing spiritually. How do I connect my spiritual growth with my work?

- I'm in a major transition (graduation, marriage, new job or job loss, divorce, illness, death of a loved one). How do I find meaning and direction?

- I have enough outer success. How do I find inner fulfillment?

This book was developed by interviewing older adults about such deep questions, then combining their wisdom with my studies in the fields of adult development and counseling psychology. Specifically, I asked a cross-section of older adults this question: "If you could live your life over again, what would you do differently?"

Three themes wove their way through all the interviews. The respondents consistently said they would be

- more reflective,

- more courageous,

- clear earlier about purpose.

From these interviews, I concluded that purpose naturally resides deep inside the human soul. All people seem to have a natural desire and capacity to contribute somehow to life. Each of us wants to leave footprints. And each of us has a unique purpose. Each of us is an experiment of one. We can learn from, but not adopt the purpose of, another person; we must unlock our own. Each of us is on a lifelong quest to find our purpose, whether we are consciously pursuing the quest or are vaguely aware that something is missing.

The quest for unlocking your purpose begins with believing you have one. No book, of course, can convince you of this. You must arrive at your own decision. But, the process works if you work the process. And, many people today are doing just that. Unlocking your purpose is not a single revelation; it is a process that must be experienced.

What Is the Purpose Movement?

Over the past decade, there's been an explosion of the interest in purpose. Psychologists describe it as the pathway to happiness. Scientists point to it as essential to brain health and well-being. Business experts make the case that purpose is a key to exceptional productivity and organizational credibility, and medical professionals have found that people with purpose in their lives are less prone to disease and even live longer.

Throughout history, humans have sought to make sense of their lives, searching for meaning through prayer, retreat, art, music, nature, community, gratitude, forgiveness, and multiple other ways. Traditionally, purpose was connected with the spiritual aspect of people's lives, and healers, priests, and shamans were the ministers who helped people connect with the sacred to restore bodies and souls to health and wholeness. Now science is increasingly validating what people have known all along: that purpose is fundamental. When it comes to life's inevitable breakdowns, purpose can provide a breakthrough. Purpose can give us the will to live. Without purpose, we can die. With purpose, we can live in dignity and compassion. Purpose is the one thing that cannot be taken from us.

Indeed, I believe that the process of unlocking your purpose and finding the courage to live it—what I call the power of purpose—is the single most important developmental task we can undertake today.

The twenty-first century shift to an accelerated, global, technology-driven world is driving a purpose movement. Such periods tend to spotlight what does not change—what remains constant and nonnegotiable in our lives. Purpose is one of those constants. People of all ages are seeking a new perspective on how they fit into this changing world. We are challenged to find relevant answers to the age-old questions of purpose and meaning. In this era, purpose has the marks of a movement—an inner-directed quest. We could say that we are living in the Purpose Age.

In addition, many of us have come to acknowledge publicly what we privately knew all along: that surviving adolescence and early adulthood did not ensure a tranquil, jolt-free passage through the rest of our careers and lives. We change; our priorities and values shift; confidence grows, dissolves into doubt, returns; relationships evolve, break apart, reform; careers and lifestyles lose energy or take on new interest—all forming a complex life cycle. Thus, purpose is not discovered once and then we are done with it. It is reimagined at various points throughout the life cycle, typically during crises and major life transitions.

Welcome to the Third Edition

The Third Edition is different. Here's why. As a lifelong student of purpose, I've kept learning and growing. The insights in this book have grown along with me. The lessons learned have come from study, practice, and stories from past readers. Like a good school or teacher, we can return to a good book over and over for lifelong learning. Like most of us, the purpose story has grown and matured. And, parts of the story have stayed the same.

I initially chose to write this book because of my deep personal belief that we live in an evolving spiritual world and that every individual in this world has unique gifts and a purpose to use those gifts to contribute value to the world.

This book builds on earlier editions of *The Power of Purpose,* expanding and deepening the conversation. It is based on forty years of study and experiences with people of all ages who were engaged in the purpose quest. New stories about purpose have been added, and other material has been updated. In addition, the Resources at the back of the book have been updated for the many people who asked me how to use the book in seminars, classes, book clubs, and spiritual or study groups.

The book is organized in a way that makes sense to me, but everyone has different needs and interests, so you should feel free to follow any order you want.

I believe that spirit touches and moves our lives through the purpose journey. That is my starting point for helping people to unlock their purpose. In a pluralistic society, not everyone will agree with that starting point. That's all right. Let me be clear, however, that my objective is not intended to express a specific religious point of view or to exclude people who don't believe as I do. Instead, this starting point is the very reason for my acceptance of the many differences among people. Because of my starting point, I believe that each person has a spiritual reason for being and that our world is incomplete until each one unlocks her or his purpose.

I hope you will find your purpose—if I have found mine, this book will be a catalyst for you finding yours.

Richard J. Leider
Minneapolis, Minnesota

PART I

What Is Your Purpose?

CHAPTER 1

The Purpose Checkup

〜

I was just trying to get home from work.

ROSA PARKS

What is your purpose? We all have a unique gift and were put on this earth to share it. What is yours?

The first step toward unlocking your purpose is to mine your life story for major threads and themes that reveal your lifelong gifts, passions, and values. Next, create a clear purpose statement that energizes you to get up each morning with intention and joy. The words in your purpose statement must be yours. They must capture your essence. And they must call you to action each and every day. You must envision the impact you'll have on your world as a result of living your purpose. Your actions—not your words—are, ultimately, what truly matters.

To do this, let's begin with a Purpose Checkup. Many of us accept the wisdom of regular physical checkups. We're also generally willing to review our financial situation with some regularity.

So, if money and medical checkups are essential, we might be wise to take guidance from the financial

and medical worlds and adopt the practice of a regular meaning checkup on that third dimension to ensure
that our spirit—our sense of purpose—remains healthy.

The Purpose Checkup

Take a moment, now, and complete the Purpose Checkup (in the Resource section at the end of the book). Use
this checkup to check in with yourself yearly, perhaps on
your birthday!

Purpose is essential to our well-being. It is what
makes us human. Purpose is not only what makes us
human, it gives us the will to live or to persevere. It
gives us a reason to get up in the morning. Purpose
is fundamental to our health, healing, happiness, and
longevity.

Purpose is one of the chief requisites for a well-lived
life. A constant in the lives of people who experience a
sense of well-being are the moments of meaning—the
"purpose moments." This chapter shows the importance of purpose moments and helps you to recognize
and create such moments in your own life.

The Power of Purpose Moments

Most of us want to know there is a purpose to life—that
our being here does mean something and that what we
do matters. Most of us want our lives to matter, and we
want to live intentionally.

Rosa Parks had a purpose moment that ultimately
changed a nation. She was arrested for refusing to give

up her bus seat to a white passenger in Montgomery, Alabama, on December 1, 1955. This single act of intention sparked a bus boycott that led to the integration of Alabama's bus system and paved the way for the civil rights movement in the United States.

Meaning matters. The search for meaning is basic to us all. However, we often examine it only when some crisis forces us to confront it—an arrest, an illness, a death, a divorce, or a loss of job. We take life for granted until a crisis wakes us up and forces us to ask the big questions. Crisis is a catalyst for purpose moments. And purpose moments bring us face-to-face with the big questions, such as What am I meant to do here?

Flight 427 was scheduled to depart Chicago's O'Hare Airport at 4:50 p.m. on a hectic Friday afternoon. Bill was on his way to Pittsburgh to attend his first meeting of the executive committee of a college board of trustees. Just before flight time, above the din of a busy O'Hare, Bill heard a page that asked him to check with the nearest gate agent. He was instructed to call his office immediately, where he learned that his meeting had been canceled—the first such cancellation in eleven years!

Shortly before Flight 427 was to begin boarding, Bill turned in his boarding pass and made a quick exit to another concourse, where his assistant, Nancy, had booked him on a flight back to his hometown of Atlanta. When he called his wife, Valerie, on his mobile phone from his car on the way home, he was greeted by an outburst of tears and raw emotion. "Bill," she sobbed, "You haven't heard! The plane you were supposed to be on to Pittsburgh crashed short of the airport and no one survived."

Bill was stunned. Of that purpose moment on the freeway, he said, "There was only this amazing calm, a sense of peace that settled over me and affirmed that God was holding me in the palm of His hand." He arrived home to tears of joy and hugs that didn't want to quit, while the television brought the bitter details of Flight 427 into their living room. "I know my reprieve is temporary. My life has been extended for now."

Bill believes that God had something more for him to do with his life. On Monday after his narrow escape, he got a hint of what that purpose might be. At his insurance agency, where he was managing director, he was besieged by friends, staff, and agents, all expressing gratitude for his role in their lives. Bill was already the leader of one of the largest, most successful insurance agencies in the country, but at that moment he realized that his true purpose, from here on, was to "grow values-driven people." That became the purpose of his life and agency. Bill no longer postponed those purpose moments but focused his newly precious time on coaching people to live in alignment with their values.

A Whole Life

Our well-being and quality of life depend on finding greater wholeness in life. The words health, heal, whole, and holy all derive from the same root. This reveals the obvious fact that to grow whole is not just a challenge of money and health, but a challenge of meaning as well.

Having a purpose in life—a clear reason to get up in the morning—is essential to growing whole. Imagine that you've decided to conduct your own personal survey by asking a handful of your friends, What is a life purpose? What do you guess the most common answer might be? Would it be similar to your own response or quite different?

At first glance, it might seem like the answer to the question is so obvious that it's a waste of your time to even ask it. Don't be fooled, however. There is wisdom in revisiting the questions that we think we already know how to answer. Our answers change at different phases of our lives and with changing life circumstances.

I've dedicated my professional life to exploring that single question. Consequently, I've had the privilege of asking thousands of people that question and many others. I've discovered that the majority of people define life purpose in a similar way. They may use different words, but the common thread weaving through their responses is this: "A life purpose is what I'm meant to do and be with my whole life."

Living a Life Worth Living

So, what is your purpose? Whether we explore this question publicly or privately, it is vital to our health, healing, wholeness, and our holiness that we do examine the question. Because what ultimately shapes our lives are the questions we ask, fail to ask, or never dream of asking. It is our questions that shape our humanity.

If we had to name what makes life worth living, what gives it meaning and purpose, most of us would probably say it's the people we love. Relationships, along with work, are the core differences in quality of life at all ages. Whom we love and how we love them are in a way the fundamental reasons we get up in the morning.

Yet the number-one issue in many people's lives today is isolation. A sense of aloneness—a strong feeling of isolation or going it alone—affects almost half of us. We complain that we either want more time for friends or would like to have more true friends, versus acquaintances, because busy lives can result in an abundance of acquaintances and a poverty of true friends.

We can easily fill our lives with busyness. There is always more to be done, always a way to keep from staring into the mirror. If we're not careful, we can begin to mistake our busyness for meaning, turning our lives into a checklist of to-dos that can occupy all the waking hours of our days and leave us breathless, with our feeling of friendship left incomplete.

And always there is more to do. Our to-do lists will outlive us. The labors of our lives will be endless. For every person who summons up the focus and energy to step out on the purpose quest, there are many more who plod on, waiting—waiting for some magical, easy solution to their quest, waiting to live the life they yearn for, a life that matters.

Discovering What Matters

The Met Life Mature Market Institute (MMI) applied sophisticated market research to the question of purpose. The MMI team worked closely with me and used my purpose work as a foundation for the purpose model in this study. The study, titled Discovering What Matters, explored with a researcher's eye for precision the way people prioritize their lives as they face transitions. This marriage of measurement to meaning produced unique, measurable evidence about the role purpose plays in people's lives. It revealed that regardless of age, gender, financial status, or life phase, the majority of people assign the most importance to meaning-related activities and, above all else, spending time with friends and family.

People with a sense of purpose in their lives were more likely to report being "happy" and to describe themselves as living the "good life." Having a sense of purpose was related to possessing both a "focus" on essential things today, and a "vision" of the future they wanted to enjoy.

The study showed that the concept of purpose, even the word itself, is something held in high regard by many, perhaps even most people. Some described purpose as giving them a general direction for their lives, while others even went so far as to allow it to prioritize the key choices required in their day-to-day living. And yet, many of the respondents might have found it difficult to honestly point to how they would use purpose in the daily choices they make.

But is purpose merely a luxury that is nice to have, or a more powerful fundamental concept? Responses revealed that purpose was the differentiator between those who reported living the "good life" and those not living the good life. Eighty-four percent of those who felt their lives had purpose reported that they were living the good life.

Build-Your-Own Life

A build-your-own trade-off exercise was used to assess people's expectations of what their lives would be like with respect to activities five years in the future. They were given a set number of "life points" to distribute among a range of activities in four categories: money, medicine, meaning, and place. Consistent with results from other parts of the study, respondents across all age groups allocated the most life points to meaning-related activities—that is, being with friends and family—with older respondents (aged sixty-five to seventy-four) focusing the most time on meaning-related activities.

It is clear from this research that the pursuit of meaning and purpose in our lives is fundamental, and that the older people are, the more important living with meaning and purpose becomes. While there are certainly some differences among age, income, and asset levels, the consistent message from this research is that the circumstances that truly bring a sense of well-being to life are fairly universal.[1]

Everyone Else Has a Purpose. So What's Mine?

An entertaining evocation of this purpose research is the musical *Avenue Q,* which is the twenty-first longest-running show in Broadway history and has won several Tony Awards, including the award for best musical. The show has also spawned other productions around the globe, including the one I experienced at the Gielgud Theatre in London.

The show is largely inspired by (and is in the style of) *Sesame Street.* Most of the characters in the show are puppets operated by actors onstage; the set depicts several tenements on a rundown street in an outer borough of New York City. However, the characters are in their twenties and thirties and face adult problems instead of those faced by preschoolers, thus making the show more suited for the adults who grew up with Sesame Street. A recurring theme is the central character's search for his elusive "purpose."

I sat enthralled as the song *Purpose* was sung. The core message—everyone else has a purpose, so, what's mine?—brought forth murmurs from the strangers sitting around me, as they chuckled over the lyrics, such as "Purpose, it's the little flame that lights a fire under your ass./Purpose, it's like driving a car with a full tank of gas," and others. I left the theater that night feeling affirmed that purpose had truly arrived on the public stage. From shows in London and New York, from youngsters and oldsters, the ever-elusive purpose-in-life theme was finally on the marquee. *Avenue Q* was a purpose moment for me.

Purpose helps us understand what is core to our life, what we care about in our actual day-to-day living. Our world suddenly comes to life.

The Most Memorable Mentor I Ever Met

One person who had a profound purpose-moment effect on my life was Dr. Richard Gustavovich Reusch, my college advisor. On the first day of class of my first day at college, a short, bald man walked in dressed in a green and tan checked sport coat over a maroon vest, black tie, British cavalry twill trousers, and well-shined cordovan shoes. He was not what I expected! He silently looked the class over as if he were a drill sergeant assessing new recruits. He then began class, speaking in a heavy accent. To this day, I can cite stories from his "world religions" lectures verbatim.

Dr. Reusch required students to pick up their exams in his office so he could check in with each one. More than test grades were the subject of discussions in his office, however. At the end of my first semester of college, in danger of flunking out, I went to talk to Dr. Reusch after final exams. I can still smell the pipe smoke and picture his office, where he was surrounded by African artifacts collected in his forty years of calling as a "Maasai missionary" in Tanzania. He was the best story teller I'd ever heard.

"I'm really lost," I told him. "I want to stay here, but I've really screwed up my life. What should I do?"

Dr. Reusch was unlike any other professor on campus. His compassion changed my life. He didn't ask about my courses but simply asked me to tell him something about myself. "About myself?" No other professor had ever asked me that! A magical hour later, I left his office with a new sense of what I wanted in school and in life. Somehow, Dr. Reusch made the hour almost a spiritual experience, and I felt something special was intended for my life.

Twenty years later I traveled to Tanzania and climbed Mount Kilimanjaro. I was astonished to learn that the crater at the summit is named Reusch Crater. Dr. Reusch climbed Mount Kilimanjaro sixty-five times, helped to establish its exact altitude, and discovered the crater now officially named after him. He knew twenty languages and he wrote books on religion, history, and geography in German, English, and Swahili.

After learning about Reusch Crater, I went back to Tanzania to find out more about Dr. Reusch. Upon interviewing people who knew him, I was amazed to learn that his life story read like Lawrence of Arabia. He was an Oriental scholar, university professor, Lutheran pastor, political refugee, East African missionary, mountaineer, ethnographer, spy, linguist, historian, and "honorary Maasai warrior!" Suddenly, I realized that my advisor had sparked the interest of reporters in the world beyond our campus. He was, in fact, memorable. Dr. Reusch came to Minnesota and taught college courses in church history, comparative religion, and fencing. His archive files are stuffed with letters of appreciation from young people like me, from parents of students, and from Maasai leaders in Tanzania, who said, "Come, please, and help us again."

He concluded his ministry of service at a small, rural church. Two weeks before he died, he announced his resignation date. That date became the occasion of his funeral.

Dr. Reusch used to say that a miracle occurred when a need and a solution converged. That day in his office I witnessed a miracle, thanks to a life memorably lived. He was one of the most purposeful people I have ever crossed paths with. His purpose was "Loyalty is what counts in life!" It was shaped by the book of Revelation: "Be you loyal unto death and I will give you the crown of life."

Purpose is the recognition of the "loyalty in life." Purpose defines our legacy. And, his was evident. It may find expression through family, community, relationship, work, and spiritual activities. We receive from life what we are loyal to.

Look ahead. How old do you think you'll live to be? Imagine you're that age. As you look back on your life, what would you like to be able to say is your legacy? How did you become the person you were destined to be? What might you do to create purpose moments so that you can look back over your life with "loyalty?"

CHAPTER 2

The Purpose Myths

〜

Service is the rent we pay for living. It is the very purpose of life, and not something you do in your spare time.
MARIAN WRIGHT EDELMAN

"Let Life Question You!"

Viktor Frankl, Holocaust survivor, therapist, and author of *Man's Search for Meaning,* was another person who profoundly impacted my life. Frankl noted that many of us are questioning life, and suggested instead, "Let life question you!" We ask: What has life done for me? Will things go my way today? What's in it for me? However, there is a more powerful wisdom in reversing the questioning and letting life question us. An openness to being questioned by life is a way to unlock our purpose. It is often in the midst of profound purpose moments that we pull back from the entanglements of daily survival and let life question us. The benefit of a crisis is often the letting go of petty concerns, conflicts, and the need for control and the realization that life is short and every moment precious.

Cancer therapists Carl and Stephanie Simonton give their patients this advice:

You must stop and reassess your priorities and values. You must be willing to be yourself, not what people want you to be because you think that is the only way you can get love. You can no longer be dishonest. You are now at a point where, if you truly want to live, you have to be who you are.[2]

Could there be any better advice for us?

Whenever we are confronted with a purpose moment, such as cancer or a fate that is unavoidable, we are given the choice to let life question us. What matters is the attitude we take toward the situation. This chapter will help you learn to let life question you.

A Marathon of Hope

A sense of purpose is rarely handed to us. We get it by choosing it, by choosing to say, "Yes, I matter; I want my life to matter." Because a sense of purpose comes from within, only we know if we have it. Only we are aware if something in our life makes us want to get up in the morning.

Terry Fox[3] is a clear example. For this young Canadian, the necessity to unlock his purpose was thrust upon him early in life. Two days after his eighteenth birthday, Terry learned he had a cancerous tumor in his right knee. His leg would have to be amputated immediately because the cancer could spread through the rest of his body. Suddenly, life was tentative, no longer to be taken for granted. Despite the shock and the speed with which

Terry's life had changed, he spent little time in the trap of self-pity. Within the confines of his hospital room, Terry detected a purpose moment, his personal reason to live.

Many of us will be forced to reflect upon the reason for our existence when we experience severe crises. But as Terry Fox put it, "You don't have to do like I did—wait until you lose a leg or get some awful disease—before you can take the time to find out what kind of stuff you're made of. Start now. Anybody can."

Two weeks after his surgery, Terry began chemotherapy. The cancer clinic and the painful treatments were a reminder to Terry that almost half of all cancer patients never recover. He began to detect what he cared deeply about, what moved him. He decided to do something for the people who were still in the hospital. Terry began to unlock a new sense of purpose, which crystallized into a specific project: He would run all the way across Canada to raise one million dollars to fight cancer and would give the money to the Canadian Cancer Society.

The power of purpose had transformed an average athlete into a person who ran a marathon a day for five months with an artificial leg! After completing three-fifths of the journey across Canada, Terry Fox had to leave his Marathon of Hope. He never finished because the cancer had spread to his lungs. But by the time of his death, one year later, he had surpassed his goal. He had raised many millions of dollars and had inspired hundreds of thousands of people. Life questioned Terry and he answered.

Terry Fox symbolized what most of us want to believe—that there is purpose to life, that our being here does mean something, that what we do does matter. The sheer determination of one individual can turn a seemingly mediocre idea into a stunning success. The lesson for us is that behind the creation of any great deed is at least one individual who was consumed by a purpose to make a difference. And the only place we can find this kind of motivation is within.

Four Purpose Myths

If you feel inclined to dismiss Terry Fox's story as bigger than life with no practical application for your own life, you may be subscribing to some commonly held myths about purpose.

It's not just the high achievers but people who achieve less dramatic successes as well—all the people in this book—who have to overcome their self-imposed doubts and other obstacles to get started when they discover what moves them. The following are four common myths that may block us from experiencing the power of purpose. As you read each one, ask yourself, Do I believe this?

Myth 1: To have purpose means I must do something completely original.

Reality: Can you think of anything that is totally new? Almost every idea or creation is an extension or builds on previous ideas. New scientific breakthroughs are built on existing fundamental truths, often as the result of reorganizing or reapplying old concepts. As we unlock our purpose, we often need to accept this fact: At the heart, most new ideas result from borrowing, adding, combining, or modifying old ones. Like runners in a relay race, we simply carry the baton another leg of the race.

Action: The paradox of purpose is that in order to address new solutions to problems, we must first familiarize ourselves with the ideas of others to form a base for launching our own ideas. Gather as much information as you can (realizing that you'll never have enough). Make a decision. Get on with the choice to live with purpose.

Myth 2: Only a few special people have true purpose in their lives.

Reality: This is the most commonly rationalized of all myths. There is no denying that often we have relied on saints, sages, and experts to solve many of our problems. However, history is filled with extraordinary contributions made by ordinary people who had virtually no expertise in the areas where they made their mark. In fact, being a novice is often an asset because we aren't hemmed in by traditional ways of viewing a situation.

Action: Purpose appears and is powerful in proportion to the energies we expend rather than to our degree of expertise. It's the passion to make a difference that counts most, so we must ignite our passion.

Myth 3: True purpose comes as inspiration or revelation. Until that time comes, I might as well keep plodding ahead.

Reality: The "pop-in" theory of purpose would have us believe that creative ideas and new directions are flashes of brilliance or revelations that suddenly appear to the fortunate—purpose descends on the lucky few. If we believe that, nothing will happen for sure! Most successful people can attest to the absurdity of waiting to be inspired.

Action: Act first. Reflect second. Inspiration comes to those who act on it. First we begin, then purpose moments appear everywhere.

Myth 4: Purpose is a luxury. I need to make a living!

Reality: Many times we become so caught in day-to-day survival activity that we lose sight of why we're doing it, and our activity becomes a false end in itself rather than a meaningful means to an end. Henry David Thoreau put it bluntly: "It isn't enough to be busy. Ants are busy." The question we should ask ourselves is What are we busy about? "Gee, I'd love to get involved, but who's got the time? I have a spouse, job, children, and financial commitments. How on earth can you expect me to find the time?" Sound familiar? For most of us, time is indeed the bigger barrier. But waiting until we have the time is as futile as trying to save money by putting away what we don't happen to spend.

Action: The only way to commit time to purpose is to steal it from some other activity. This is what the power of purpose is all about—aligning our energies around our true priorities.

Finding Goals and Something Else

Terry Fox had a personal impact on my own life. While camping around the perimeter of Lake Superior, I came upon Terry Fox running just outside of Thunder Bay, Ontario. Sandwiched between the flashing red lights of a highway patrol car and the van with a Marathon of Hope banner on its side was Terry Fox—with a look in his eyes that is etched indelibly in my mind. That look of determination was the power of purpose in action. The unexpected meeting planted the seed that led to the writing of this book.

He challenged me with that look. He made me ask, "What is life asking of me?"

Ever since I was a child, I've had an intense curiosity about what motivates people. I've always felt convinced that there could be more to my life if only I could find it. Tempted by the glowing promises of self-help books, I read them all, and they all said, "The first step is to decide what your goals in life are." So I sat down cheerfully one day, with pencil in hand to jot down my goals. They didn't come!

The self-help books had suggested that I should want specific goals such as success and to earn a certain amount of money. But none of these goals moved me. I was unable to find the clear purpose Terry Fox had, the purpose that would make my goals meaningful. I was beginning to question whether there might be something wrong with me.

Whenever I did manage to commit myself to a goal, I found I achieved more success than I ever expected, but the results never brought me the fulfillment the books promised. I had never been able to find in one of those goals a meaningful aim for my life. On one day, a certain goal would be important; on another day, a different goal would capture my fancy. I rarely committed myself to anything passionately. I wanted to work for a purpose, not just for a living or for one goal after another.

Embracing Purpose before Goals

In describing people like Terry Fox, who have unlocked a sense of purpose, I once felt a certain amount of uneasiness. I didn't want to describe a goal that seemed so unrealistic, so ideal. Purpose had always meant goals to me, but Terry Fox got me thinking again. I started to realize that goals were not the same as purpose, and that I needed to embrace the "why?" of purpose before I selected the "what?" of my goals. I began again, this time to shape a purpose for my life. And it was no longer the shaping of life to fit my ego-driven goals but rather the gradual detecting of a purpose outside myself.

Terry Fox showed the true joy I sought for my own life. He was alive! I realized that it is not our specific goals that create this aliveness; rather, it is the sense of purpose with which we embrace the goals.

People like Terry Fox have learned to let life question them and have moved the focus of their attention and concern away from themselves to others.

Purpose, then, is not a job or a role or a goal. It is our aim—the belief that our lives, our part in the whole of things, truly matters. Having a profound sense of the "why?" we're doing it drives the will to do it. It is thus a mindset, a choice. It is first and foremost the choice to choose "life" despite the circumstances we find ourselves in. It is the choice to bring who we are—our gifts and energies—to whatever we are doing.

One purpose in life is not more important than another. There is purpose whenever we use our gifts and talents to respond to something we believe in, something larger than ourselves.

You Were Not Born for Nothing

It may or may not be a new idea that you were born for a reason, for some purpose. If you have never considered the idea that you have a life purpose, now is the time to decide that you're going to look at life in a new way for a while. You might even question your own skepticism because you are now curious about this notion that you were born for a reason.

You may be one of the many who has always felt inside that there is something you were meant to do with your life, and you would be very happy to live with a purpose if only you could find it.

Whatever your present position about purpose,

relax. There is a place deep inside you that is yearning to believe that you were born for something.

The reason many people have difficulty in believing that life has a purpose is because they do not see themselves as large enough. Thinking larger about yourself means coming to terms with the fact that, whether you concur or not, it makes a difference that you are living this life. You may never have experienced a large purpose moment like Terry Fox did, but still it makes a difference that you are alive, living this moment on this earth. Thinking large simply means you are willing to embrace the possibility of purpose—that you realize that you contribute something special.

It's about Unlocking Something You Already Have

The great thing about your life purpose is that you already have it, and you already know many things about it. You're not going to uncover some unsuspected thing about yourself that you could never do.

Unlocking your life purpose is really a process of self-awareness and choice. It may be, as it is for many people, that you have so discounted your gifts that you have lost sight of your most valuable assets. You may believe that only special people, like Terry Fox, can find and have a purpose, and you have never considered yourself special.

Whatever your thoughts might have been, now you can think about yourself in a new way. You can acknowledge that something about you is unique, special. You can feel your life is as significant as anyone else's, and you can act on that fact. You can choose how you want to live, work, and relate.

When you let go of the purpose myths, you claim your power and feel that people need you and appreciate your gifts. Take time to notice the times when the purpose myths show up in life. How can you let go of them?

CHAPTER 3

The Purpose Path

〜

*We are all on a spiral path. No growth takes place
in a straight line. There will be setbacks along the
way. . . . There will be shadows, but they will be
balanced by patches of light. . . . Awareness of the
pattern is all you need to sustain you along the way.*

KRISTIN ZAMBUCKA

All life is a spiral of change, a continuous graceful curve
toward purpose. There is a definite path to it all, and we
spend our whole lives seeking to understand that path
by living with different questions at each age and phase.
Searching for the path is the heart of our human maturity. If we're aware of that path, and our place on it, we
can identify the best choices to sustain us along the way.
Most of us find that our purpose changes as experiences
change over our lifetime. A new sense of purpose may
be triggered when we reach a particular age, by a crisis,
or by a natural, ongoing discovery of what matters most
in life.

Asking new questions as we age is part of the life
quest. This chapter will help you detect your purpose
path.

The Purpose Path

If living on purpose sounds like an impractical order, think about a spiral. The Random House Unabridged Dictionary of the English Language defines a spiral as "running continually around a fixed point or center while constantly receding from or approaching it." The spiral projects the image of a continuity that coils in one plane around one particular center. There is a clear analogy between the path of purpose and the pattern of a spiral staircase; each has a basic center of orientation that provides a coherent pattern. Think of your life as a spiral staircase, with many steps behind you and many ahead.

The spiral is a natural pattern for understanding our purpose. As we, too, move through different phases, our purpose changes. The old phases feel cramped and lack room to stretch and breathe. We outgrow people, places, and purposes. We move on to new phases to make way for the new growth to emerge.

As Pat Murphy and William Neill see it in their book *By Nature's Design:* "Life more often than not does not draw straight lines. The world is filled with graceful curves—from the elegant spiral in the heart of the nautilus shell to the twisting double helix of DNA that codes for the nautilus' growth."[4]

We do not remain children forever but rather move through various life phases toward wisdom and maturity. As we move through each phase of our own path of growth, we naturally look in different directions and ask different questions. Each phase of our life has its own special questions, and the way we answer the questions determines our path.

Life is a continuous quest of questions to be answered and lessons to be learned. We grow through phases of progressive awakenings that involve physical, mental, emotional, and spiritual insights.

If you look back and examine the past phases of your life, each contained natural, yet core, questions. And as you lived in the core questions, they taught you the essential truths of life and showed you new questions.

The secret to a fully alive life is learning how to reframe our questions, letting go of what is no longer relevant, and taking on new questions guided by our growing wisdom. Each phase is naturally important as a basis for further growth.

Purpose As an Improvisatory Art

Each transition to a new phase of purpose is accompanied by a time of uncertainty, a chaotic period of time in which we recalibrate around a new core question. In fact, our phases may never seem quite predictable, may not follow a plan that we might have imagined or expected. Perhaps rather than using words such as developments, stages, or phases, we might consider another word: improvisations.

Anthropologist Mary Catherine Bateson observed in her book *Composing a Life* that the adult years are not linear but fluid and even disjointed. She wrote:

The model of an ordinary successful life that is held up for young people is one of early decision and commitment, often to an educational preparation that launches a single rising trajectory. . . . Many of societies' casualties are men and women who assumed they had chosen a path in life and found that it disappeared in the underbrush.[5]

Bateson saw adult life as "an improvisatory art" combining familiar and unfamiliar components in response to new situations.

One reason for the improvisatory nature of life now may be that a growing number of people are expecting their path to provide daily meaning as well as their daily bread. They want work that integrates their unique gifts and talents with the practical realities of surviving and making a living.

After graduating from college, my son, Andrew Leider, like many young people, wanted both meaning and money. "What's your purpose?" I asked Andrew over coffee one morning. He quickly responded, "To make my way in the world without losing myself!"

Andrew never intended to live what he called a "tract life" after college. He was not looking for what he'd do for the next forty years. While many of his friends were becoming lawyers, doctors, ministers, and businesspeople, he was enjoying a different quest and different questions. His core question was, "What am I willing to trade my time for without compromising my values?"

Because of his passion for adventure, he gravitated to work for the wilderness-based Outward Bound schools. The purpose of Outward Bound is to conduct safe, adventure-based programs structured to inspire self-esteem, self-reliance, concern for others, and care for the environment. As an Outward Bound instructor and, eventually Program Director, Andrew studied intensely and uncovered a natural gift for creating, designing, and leading learning programs. He found that "Outward Bound fulfills my personality for the predictable future. Although I'm not making much money, I am able to survive nicely and integrate who I am with what I do."

Outward Bound ran its natural course for Andrew. After ten years, a new vision was coming clearer, and it was time to improvise. The next phase combined a Somatic Coach Certification with his program design, management, and leadership skills. As executive director of Montana Yellowstone Expeditions, he was able to follow a deeper call to help youth find their way in the world.

The power of this work for Andrew was that it was a place that consciously supported the integration of his work and his life. It gave him the opportunity to improvise—to bring his whole self to work and to experience the integrity of working without compromising his values.

Today, Andrew's life has, once again, moved into a new phase with new questions and new possibilities. As a coach and consultant to organizations like Outward Bound and many others, he has created a work style that gives him the freedom to spend precious time with his rapidly growing young daughter, Eleanor.

"One in a Million"

The late management consultant Peter Drucker said about career choices: "The probability that the first choice you make is right for you is roughly one in a million. If you decide that your first choice was the right one, chances are you are just plain lazy."[6] This should not be discouraging because everything we do builds on the evolution of our purpose. Rarely do we have wasted work, though at the time it might seem that way. We're always growing and mastering life's lessons—even hard-to-recognize ones—that move us forward on the purpose path.

We're all challenged to improvise and create the specific and unique path we are going to tread. It takes courage to make what we do reflect who we are. Yet we are often not encouraged to do that. From early childhood, we are taught to behave in ways that fit the purposes of others. As children, we are naturally open yet dependent on the lead set by others. Following the lead of our parents, peers, teachers, and others brings approval. Sooner or later, we realize it is easier to base our choices on what is expected of us rather than on what is meaningful to us. Sometimes we become so dependent on these external standards that we no longer know what we truly need or want.

Instead of improvising and continuing to take risks on our purpose path, many of us postpone and wait for something to happen. We wait for the revelation, when our full gifts and talents will be unleashed and used, not committing ourselves to anything until everything is right. Waiting by its very nature traps us in a way of living that makes our life feel superficial and disappointing. We become stalled on our purpose path.

If we do not unlock our purpose, then a large portion of each day is spent doing something we might not truly care about and would rather not be doing. We may spend so much of our lives waiting that we miss the true joy of life and remain unfulfilled. The day will come. Death will claim us, and we will not have had more than a moment of contentment.

Purpose Is Immortal

One of the requirements of unlocking our purpose is to come face-to-face with our own mortality. To do that, we must make friends with death. Living purposefully means facing squarely the question of mortality.

Mary Foley's life was ended before she was able to complete her journey. Mary believed deeply in human potential, and she believed in herself. As corporate manager of health services for a major manufacturing company, Mary was one of those rare mentors who consistently held positive expectations of people and encouraged them to not settle for less than their higher purpose. Her purpose was "to be a positive influence on the lives of women and children." Mentoring other women in her field was the work she loved. By believing in the dreams of other young professional women, Mary unlocked her purpose and shared her own struggles and questions.

Mary frequently checked on what people were reading, talked about what she was reading, and often recommended or gave books to others. She discovered an earlier edition of this book and gave it to many people. She inquired and was genuinely interested in people's purpose path.

Tragically, Mary was murdered. Her life was snuffed out at an early age. Mary had helped many young women find their path. She played her part in creating the kind of world she dreamed of. An organization called the Friends of Mary Foley keeps her purpose alive in the community. Every year since her death, a group of her friends get together on her birthday to celebrate and toast her life. Each year they raise money and resources for a cause that aligns with Mary's purpose. One of her friends said, "She lived with more purpose than most anyone I have known." Her purpose is immortal.

Did My Life Matter?

People like Mary help us ask the questions that are meaningful and life enhancing at any phase of our lives. In childhood we ask, Who am I? In adolescence, the question becomes, What do I want to be when I grow up? In young adulthood we want to know, What is my calling? In "midlife" we mull over, What's it all about? In young older adulthood, the question becomes, How do I grow whole, not old? In "elderhood" we ask, What's my legacy?

If we embrace these questions, our answers will be satisfying when we look back over our lives and ask such questions as, "Did my life matter?" We will feel few regrets. In contrast, when we have no purpose, we wander aimless through life, fail to realize our full potential, and sometimes look back with regrets over wasted time and opportunities.

Viktor Frankl, the Jewish psychiatrist who survived the horrors of the Nazi concentration camps, taught me the importance of finding purpose and meaning. He claimed that it was the key to survival when his choices were few and the future seemed hopeless. He and other prisoners who maintained a sense of meaning or purpose in life were the ones who were able to transcend the brutal and desperate circumstances of the camps until they were liberated. Frankl attributed his own and others' survival to the power of having a sense of purpose that kept their focus on what truly mattered.

Purpose can help us survive challenges and actually thrive as we live a life of no regrets.

Ernest Becker in *The Denial of Death* claims, "The fear of death is the basic fear that influences all others; a fear from which no one is immune no matter how disguised it may be."[7] To face death squarely is to face purpose squarely. Mysteriously, the creative spirit of the universe calls us at various times and in various ways to make our own difference in the work of the universe—to matter.

Look back over the phases of your own life path. What were your questions during each decade of your life? What is your question today? What are you obsessing about?

CHAPTER 4

The Purpose Gift

~

Service is not possible unless it is rooted in love and nonviolence. The best way to find yourself is to lose yourself in the service of others.

MAHATMA GANDHI

Life purpose is a choice to give your gifts naturally and spontaneously. Remember those times when people you care about wanted you to share with them? Maybe they were in need and asked for your assistance. Think about what you love doing and what you want to give naturally. What do you want to give others that would make a difference for them? What is it that you do naturally, that you would like to give to others?

Your natural talents are gifts for three reasons. First, you didn't have to earn them—they came with your birth. Second, they are gifts because you get something for yourself when you give them. And third, they are gifts to others because they get something from you that is theirs to keep. This chapter will help you realize that you are uniquely gifted for serving others, and will show how your gifts can help you unlock your purpose.

Purpose Is a Call to Action

If you want to unlock your life purpose, you must think of purpose as an action in the world. What gifts do you bring to serving others? Do you awaken, inspire, ignite, support? Can you persuade, challenge, teach, coach, direct? Are you naturally moved to create, design, organize, compose, master? Can you help, befriend, listen, love, accept, share? Do you seek, heal, liberate, enable, achieve?

Your life purpose is what is unique and powerful about you, the gifts you express naturally and enjoy giving. Right now, without further work or education, you have a gift to give in the area of your life purpose. There is something that you do that comes from the inside of you that you actively want to give to others. This gift of life purpose is given to you to give away to others. Purpose means action.

Don't think too much about the answer to the following three questions—your first response will be your best:

What gift do people consistently come to you for or ask you for?

What gift do others tell you, "You're so good at that?"

What gift do you truly enjoy doing—you lose all track of time in the doing of it?

"Reverence for Life"

Late one afternoon in September 1915, Albert Schweitzer was sitting on the deck of a small steamboat making its way up the Ogooue River to Lambarene in Central Africa. He was bringing medical services to the local population in French Equatorial Africa. The boat was moving cautiously through a herd of hippopotamuses in the river. As Schweitzer watched the ship's captain maneuver to avoid hitting the animals, he came to a profound realization: The captain represented the highest purpose—reverence for the life of other creatures. For years Schweitzer had been searching for his purpose in the world. He found it in Africa, and a "reverence for life."

Schweitzer recognized an expression of gifts in the care that the ship's captain was taking to avoid injuring the animals. Yet Schweitzer also observed that far more people are gifted than will admit to being so:

> Just as the rivers are much less numerous
> than underground streams, so the idealism
> that is visible is minor compared to what men
> and women carry in their hearts, unreleased
> or scarcely released. Mankind is waiting and
> longing for those who can accomplish the task
> of untying what is knotted and bringing the
> underground waters to the surface.[8]

Opportunities for aligning our lives with our gifts are virtually everywhere. Using our gifts to serve others, observed Schweitzer, leads to happiness: "The only ones among you who will be really happy are those who have sought and found how to serve."

Through the expression of our gifts, we are more

alive, just as artists are more alive when absorbed in the creation of a painting. There is a selflessness that goes with absorption in something we genuinely find interesting; yet it is also a sense of being more ourselves.

Every one of us, like Albert Schweitzer, eventually faces our own story, the time when we are challenged to define our life on this planet, our "reverence for life." Our story often surfaces when our standard answers to the big questions no longer satisfy us. Nothing shapes our lives as much as the questions we ask—or refuse to ask—throughout our lives.

How do you answer the eternal purpose question? The differences in the quality of our lives often lie in the quality of the questions that shape our stories. And without each of our stories, the story of the universe would be incomplete. My own answer to the question is still growing and deepening after many years of asking it. My life has been a history of unlocking and integrating more elements of myself into my whole life.

"Fortuitous Encounters"

On the purpose path, we may have what my friend and colleague, Larry Spears, calls "fortuitous encounters"— chance meetings with people who significantly influence our direction.

On my path to becoming a school psychologist, I became a life coach, a keynote speaker, an author, and an expedition leader. In my early twenties, I was a counseling psychology graduate student with the military draft board hounding me to complete my studies and begin my compulsory military service. In an effort to find a solution I could live with during a war I didn't support, I joined an army psychological operations reserve unit. That choice required me to leave my schooling in Colorado with my master of arts degree and return to Minnesota.

Along with the move came the necessity of supporting my family. During my job-hunting process, I "accidentally" discovered the corporate human resources field. Joining a large Fortune 100 company, I worked under a great mentor in a variety of human resource positions, ending up, after two years, as training manager. In my training role, I had the opportunity to use my coaching gifts with a large number of employees who were unclear about their career direction.

I knew from my counseling psychology training that there were many ways of helping people clarify their focus and direction. In the late 1960s, however, there were few practical books or programs available. So, I started creating my own ideas, exercises, and programs and trying them out after hours. Soon I had a growing career coaching practice after hours, a growing reputation, and a waiting list!

With a growing family and financial needs, I moved to a large bank holding company, where, in addition to a much larger human resources job, I continued to hone my career coaching skills both inside the organization and after hours. However, I still felt like a lone voice in the career wilderness.

A fortuitous encounter with Richard Bolles fueled my career coaching fires and affirmed my growing after-hours coaching practice. Dick gave me the opportunity to preview what was later to become his forty plus-year best-selling book, *What Color Is Your Parachute?* From Dick, a former Episcopalian priest, I received support for my intuitive feeling that every individual has been created with a mission in life. Dick helped me gain confidence in a belief for which I am eternally grateful: "The gifts of each of us and the value of serving others provide our mission in life." Dick sparked my interest in further studying about purpose—a passion that has guided my work and remains with me to this day.

Another fortuitous encounter, this time with author Sigurd Olson, also fed my passion about purpose. I wanted to write about purpose. As a budding writer, I had heroes and models I wanted to imitate, and Sigurd Olson was one of them.

Sigurd was a wilderness philosopher and ardent conservationist who wrote about nature and spirituality. He focused on the purpose moment that we feel when we're in the presence of nature. I was deeply moved by his writing, and his books found their way into both my backpack and my bookshelf.

I corresponded with him over several years, and he encouraged my purpose and my writing. In an essay on his own writing in his book *Open Horizons,* he wrote: "Occasionally, when I did no writing at all, my spirits fell and everything seemed without meaning or purpose."[9] The cure, he advised, was to begin again. When he began writing again, his spirit soared. He said that he wrote about things as he saw them and the passion just came through. When I was down or blocked in my writing, Sigurd inspired me to begin again, to follow my passion.

Unlocking My Purpose

During this same time period, I applied for and received a Bush Foundation Fellowship to study adult development and positive aging issues. I designed my own non-degree, customized fellowship (few programs were available at the time) in an informal arrangement with the Harvard Business School's Study of Adult Development. Through my fellowship studies, I discovered the need for and value of purpose in people's lives throughout the life span.

After my fellowship studies, I quickly chose to move into full-time career coaching work. I studied it intensely and seemed to have a natural gift for it. I launched a slowly successful coaching practice. From that start I moved to leading seminars, co-writing my first book, speaking to groups, and guiding wilderness "inventure" expeditions.

"Helping others unlock their purpose" became my purpose. It chose me. I unlocked my own purpose on the way to somewhere else. It moves me. It gets me up in the morning, excited to go to work. And it fulfills my desire to connect deeply with people's lives—to give my gifts.

As I have had the profound privilege to listen to thousands of people's stories over the last four decades, my point of view on purpose has grown. This book represents my understanding of what I have learned about unlocking the power of purpose. There are three essential tasks to unlocking purpose. To live on purpose, you must:

- Unlock your story.
- Unlock your gifts.
- Unlock your curiosity.

Unlock Your Story

Through wise teachers and elders, I became aware that we are born with a purpose. We live in a purposeful universe. Every organism in the universe has a design—a pattern that determines its function and role. A critical part of our growth is the inside-out search for that pattern. The true joy in life is to turn ourselves inside out to realize that our purpose already exists within.

Each life has a natural, built-in reason for being. That reason is to make a positive contribution to the world around it. Purpose is the creative spirit of life moving through us, from the inside out. It is the deep, mysterious direction in each of us—our path—where we have a profound intuitive sense of who we are, where we came from, where we are going, and how we might get there.

Each of us has a unique path built into our essence.

Each of us is an experiment of one. Otherwise, we would not, in our deepest moments, ask: What am I meant to do here? Our path is shaped by the inside-out questions we ask, or fail to ask, during our lives.

Unlock Your Gifts

Purpose feeds three deep spiritual hungers: to connect deeply with the power of choice in our lives; to actively know that we have a unique gift to give the world; and to use our gifts to make a contribution in some meaningful way.

Our voice in the world comes from the gifts in us, but we must unlock the gifts and choose the calling in which we express them. When we work and live with purpose, we bring together the needs of the world with our special gifts in a vocation, or calling.

Unlock Your Curiosity

Purpose is what moves us. It is the conscious choice of what, where, and how to make a positive contribution to our world. Oliver Wendell Holmes wrote, "Many people die with their music still in them."[10] Our "music" is a metaphor for the quality or passion around which we choose to express our gifts. Once we discover our music—what moves us—life takes on a new energy. Our music is so powerful that we find we can hardly refrain from moving to its rhythm. It compels us to "dance," to take action.

Our world is incomplete until each one of us

discovers what moves us. No other person can hear our music calling. We must listen and act on it for ourselves. To hear it, we need an environment that supports exploring our curiosities.

In the power of curiosity lies the purpose journey. To hear our music, we need to be curious, to listen to our deepest yearnings. The purpose journey requires the wisdom of curiosity and listening.

PART II

The Purpose Journey

CHAPTER 5

Purpose Across the Ages

∽

Ever more people today have the means
to live, but no meaning to live for.
VIKTOR FRANKL

Many people find themselves, today, in an "existential vacuum," searching for something they can devote their time and talents to. The search for meaning is especially apparent in the millennials—young people in their late twenties and thirties. The need to unlock our purpose continues across the ages, right up into retirement when we can find ourselves empty, unless we find a new purpose in life. Purpose comes early and reappears late. It's a cradle-to-grave journey. Purpose is essential to fill the vacuum. Purpose provides hope and resilience in times of drift and transition.

The Power of Choice

Viktor Frankl was a Jewish psychiatrist who spent three years during World War II living in horrific circumstances in three of the worst Nazi concentration camps.

While in the camps, Frankl realized he had one single freedom left. He had the power to choose his response to the horror around him. And so he chose to make a difference. He chose to get up every day and give others a kind word, a crust of bread, hope. He imagined his wife, Tilly, and the prospect of being with her again. He imagined finishing the book that he had been writing up to the very day he was imprisoned. He wrote it over and over in his mind and on tiny scraps of paper that he hid. He imagined himself teaching students after the war about the lessons he had learned.

Frankl survived but his family did not. Leaving the camp weighing eighty-seven pounds, he went back to Vienna to heal. When he recovered, he went on to chronicle his experiences and the insights he had drawn from them. In nine days he wrote his classic book, *Man's Search for Meaning,* which has sold more than twelve million copies in over twenty languages.

"A human being is a deciding being," he wrote. "Between stimulus and response there is a space. In that space is our power to choose our response. In our response lies our growth and our freedom."

In that space lays the power of choice. Our choices are very real and potentially life saving or life changing.

Frankl wrote, "One should not search for an abstract meaning of life. Everyone has his own vocation or mission in life to carry out a concrete assignment, which demands fulfillment."

That concrete assignment is a choice. It's a chance to answer the call to fulfill our purpose on earth. As our purpose grows over our lifetime—it is uncovered, discovered, and rediscovered—it gives our lives dignity and meaning. We are not burdened by purpose as a sense of duty or moral obligation. We care to make a difference because we recognize that it is our reason for being here.

Now science is validating what Frankl discovered— that purpose is fundamental to life. Consider the role purpose plays in helping ailments ranging from pain and depression to Alzheimer's and other diseases. Though the purpose effect remains largely shrouded in mystery, researchers now attribute some aspects to active mechanisms in the brain that influence the immune response and the will to live.

When it comes to life's inevitable breakdowns, purpose can provide breakthroughs. Purpose, as Viktor Frankl wrote, gives us the will to live—a reason to get up in the morning—regardless of our circumstances. Without purpose we can die. With purpose, we can live with choice, dignity, and meaning. Purpose is the one thing that cannot be taken from us. It enables us to survive and also to thrive.

Three Stages of Purpose

How might we harness the power of purpose to live more conscious lives and, perhaps, to even recast the most challenging situations in which we find ourselves?

There are three stages of purpose on our journey through life. What stage of purpose are you in?

Stage 1: Uncovering—"It's about me."

Purpose is perceived as coming from others, and is directed toward ourselves.

This stage begins with our birth, our family of origin, and our early experiences, challenges, and lessons learned. It is the stage that shapes us and provides us with our initial values. Our greatest crises and challenges likely shaped our purpose.

During this stage we seek to uncover our authentic pathway in life. Not just any pathway will do. Our authentic pathway is not simply one that someone will pay us to occupy (like a job or a career), nor a task we happen to have the talent to perform (like an art or a craft), nor a social role (like a parent or grandparent) in which other people will embrace us. It's got to be our own journey, one in keeping with our gifts, passions, and values.

We uncover our unique pathway by experiencing the world. We gain a sense of what is possible as well as purposeful, and we cultivate a relationship with the visible realms as much as with the hidden.

We seek to uncover the one life we can call our own. As Joseph Campbell wrote, "The differentiations of sex, age, and occupation are not essential to our character, but mere costumes which we wear for a time on the stage of the world. The image of a person within is not to be confounded with the garments. . . .Yet such designations do not tell what it is to be a person, they denote only the accident of geography, birth date and income. What is the core of us? What is the basic character of our being?"

Stage 2: Discovering—"It's about us."

Purpose is perceived as residing outside ourselves and is directed toward the needs of others.

This stage begins when we choose to make a difference in the lives of others. For most, this takes place in our current family role or work. But, this stage requires us to let go of our self-absorption and allow ourselves to be used for a larger purpose. We might not know what our larger purpose is. However, we have decided to make a small difference, one person at a time, in the lives of others. This stage gives us glimpses of an authentic life.

When we choose to make a difference in the lives of others, we begin to perceive our own lives differently, almost immediately. The right people seem to show up and the right situations seem to present themselves as opportunities to serve others. We experience the true joy in the purpose moments of life. We experience challenges that make us doubt ourselves and question our capacity. But, we wake up with a clear reason to get up in the morning.

As George Bernard Shaw wrote, "This is the true joy in life, the being used for a purpose recognized as a mighty one. . . the being a force of nature instead of a feverish selfish little clod of ailments and grievances complaining that the world will not devote itself into making you happy."

Stage 3: Rediscovering—"It's about all of us."

Purpose is perceived as coming through the self and used for the sake of all others.

This is commonly seen as a spiritual calling. We look back and see how all the phases of our lives are connected to our life today. It is the stage where our purpose becomes so clear that we can say it in a simple sentence. It's a time of larger meaning. We grow and we give. We give and we get. What we give comes back to us exponentially. We perceive ourselves as ordinary people living extraordinary lives.

We may not build libraries but we rediscover a larger purpose in reading to a child. We may not feed the homeless, but we nourish others by listening or giving a kind word. We may not start a nonprofit organization but we volunteer for something we care deeply about. We perceive how we can make a difference every day and touch the lives of everyone we meet.

The question during this stage is not what is the meaning of life, but what is life asking of us? And the answer must be chosen by each of us every day in our own way. Meaning is rediscovered in the day-to-day purpose moments when care trumps convenience.

Purpose keeps us present. When we rediscover the purpose moments, we tap into an endless supply of energy. Throughout life there is meaning available to us, and that life retains its meaning under any condition and until its final moment.

CHAPTER 6

Unlocking Your Story

〜

We can discover this meaning in life in
three different ways: [1] by doing a deed;
[2] by experiencing a value; and [3] by suffering.

VIKTOR FRANKL

Our stories make us human. Many, many years ago, when we were hunter-gatherers, we were telling one another stories. And now, hundreds of years later, we are still sharing our stories. Jonathan Gottschall, author of *The Storytelling Animal,* writes, "We are as a species, addicted to story. Even when the mind goes to sleep, the mind stays up all night telling itself stories."

Where do you start? What is your story? How do you unlock your story? Many of us are starved for alignment in our lives. Our story can serve as an aligning focus for our gifts, passions, and values. The most effective people know how to focus their daily activities while keeping their aim on a larger story, the way they want to live their lives.

The story we tell ourselves has a way of focusing time and energies around itself; that is the real power behind the story. It often helps us to refocus our lives in order to bring out our voice and full music. This chapter will help you identify your purpose story and show three ways to live it.

What Is Life Asking of You?

If we open our eyes to the world around us, we often notice the endless "needs" that life is asking us to fulfill.

- Which parts or issues of the newspaper move you?

- Which TV specials are you drawn to watch?

- Which parts of your organization's mission or strategy interest you?

- What speeches or presentations have moved you?

- Which leaders inspire you? Why?

- Which special-interest websites do you visit regularly?

- What needs of your mosque, church, synagogue, temple, or spiritual organization move you?

- What part of your political party's platform moves you?

For most of us, the community in which we live is rich with possibilities for expressing our gifts. To unlock our purpose, we need to detect—to sense—the potential issues that call us to meaningful action.

Viktor Frankl points to three pathways to meaning: "We can discover this meaning in life in three different ways: by doing a deed; by experiencing a value; and by suffering."

Three Paths to Purpose

Path 1: "Doing a Deed"

One way to start is to "notice" what's needed and wanted, and then produce it—right where we are—in our current work, family, spiritual organization, or community.

Tangible achievement and accomplishment of deeds—especially those which move us emotionally—are important. For deeds to have a real impact at a personal level, we must own the issue in a personally committed way. Claiming some deed set by others or expected of us is not nearly as satisfying. This, however, does not mean that whatever deed we select needs to be visible to others. It is "do-gooders" who need to keep score of their deeds. "Keeping score" may actually reduce our sense of contentment, as we begin to see how our commitment is driven by our own self-gratification.

Path 2: "Experiencing a Value"

We find meaning when our actions reflect what we value, what is important to us, what gifts we enjoy and want to give. If identified and clear to us, our values can guide us toward our purpose. The reverse is also true. When circumstances or our own weaknesses lead us to act counter to what we value, we feel poorly about ourselves.

Purpose calls us to live our values. Tucked away just outside the town of Osceola, Wisconsin, is a healing place. The Aveda Spa is synonymous with living our values. Nasreen Koaser, who moved from her native India to work at the spa as a hair stylist, embodied its original mission "to promote and support continuous learning as a foundation for success and well-being." Today, as a self-employed "image crafter," Nasreen brings such love and healing touch to her work that people come from long distances to fill up her calendar months and even a year in advance. In our busy, fast-paced, overscheduled world, Nasreen awaits her clients with hot herbal tea, a kind word, a healing touch, and lived values.

She strives to make people happy by helping them feel good about themselves. She says, "I love my work because I love my clients. Every day God gives me the opportunity to bring out the pure essence in my clients. That is my purpose and I am grateful for work that allows me to live my values in this way."

Rollie Larson, a ninety-four year-old retired psychologist, expresses the value of "listening" every day. He lives as a whole person, integrated in mind, body, and spirit, with the natural curiosity and enthusiasm for life of a much younger person.

Rollie states, "Purpose, for me, boils down to relationships. What goes on with me and other people, that's what gives joy to me. I tried seventeen different jobs before I found that my calling was working with people! Working with other people—sharing, caring, listening, loving—gives me a spiritual connection. Part of my prayers each night are that I can listen to someone tomorrow."

Rollie's long, esteemed counseling career took him down many paths, including founding a school counseling department, training corporate executives, opening a private practice with his late wife, Doris, and writing several books. What distinguishes Rollie is his special value—a genuine interest in listening deeply to others. His credo, "Listen to someone today," is well known to the hundreds of people he has touched over the years. He counsels people, "If you have to go through seventeen jobs to find your calling—do it! Start opening some other windows in your areas of interest. Ultimately, your work must be a turn-on; it must feel passionate."

Rollie has blended the spirit and value of listening with the maturity and wisdom of age. He has unlocked his purpose.

Andrew Greeley, quoted in Phillip Berman's book *The Courage of Conviction,* said:

> It seems to me that in the last analysis there are only two choices: Macbeth's contention that life is a tale told by an idiot, full of sound and fury and signifying nothing, and Pierre Teilhard's "something is afoot in the universe, something that looks like gestation and birth." Either there is a plan and purpose—and that plan and purpose can best be expressed by the words "life" and "love"—or we live in a cruel, arbitrary, and deceptive cosmos in which our lives are a brief transition between two oblivions.[11]

Purpose is the value we choose to center our lives around—the way we orient ourselves toward life. It is the way we make sense or meaning out of our lives. Purposeful people, like Nasreen and Rollie, choose to center their lives around the assumption that "something is afoot in the universe, something that looks like gestation and birth."

Daring to be ourselves—experiencing our values—is a challenging issue because it involves courage, which is uncomfortable for many people. And it is not something another person can do for us.

What values do you treasure and want to live in your daily life? How can you express that value today?

Path 3: "Suffering"

There are crises that eventually challenge most of us. These situations are so devastating that our entire sense of meaning may slip, leaving us shaken or enraged. At such times, feelings of shock and of feeling in limbo are not uncommon. When we cope effectively, a purpose may actually be found or strengthened or made clearer. Like Viktor Frankl, we often learn much about who we really are under conditions of "suffering." Some examples of triggering events that cause us to reassess our purpose in life include the death of a loved one; divorce or marital separation; major illness or disability; loss of work; a major geographic move; retirement; or a major financial loss.

These kinds of events cause most of us, at least temporarily, to revisit our stories. Because our life and basic sense of self are disrupted, we are reawakened to the story that we are telling ourselves.

When we are moved by something, many things previously felt to be important fade in significance. If our purpose is strong enough, it impacts all areas of our life. We begin to eliminate what is irrelevant and just so much clutter. A simplification takes place, and we achieve clarity about ourselves and our lives. We don't need to pretend to be what we're not. We recognize what is of true importance. In his seminal book *Voluntary Simplicity*, Duane Elgin quoted these remarks from Richard Gregg, who coined the term voluntary simplicity:

> Voluntary simplicity involves both inner and outer condition. It means singleness of purpose, sincerity and honesty within, as well as avoidance of exterior clutter, of many possessions irrelevant to the chief purpose of life. It means an ordering and guiding of our energy and our desires, a partial restraint in some directions in order to secure greater abundance of life in other directions. It involves a deliberate organization of life for a purpose.[12]

The way to spend our precious time and energy wisely is to know the purpose for which we live and then to change our story.

By letting go and trying a new story, we can begin to consider the possibility of new lifestyles and work styles. In the early stages of purpose, the process is one of a search for external sources of fulfillment to fill the void produced by loss. But with time, the uncertainties subside and gradually give way to hope about the future. Our priorities shift to living in new ways. As we adapt to the change and normalize our lives, we feel empowered with new confidence and competence. And we feel the deep joy of living with purpose.

What is your story, today? What are you telling yourself about what truly matters in your life? How can you live your own story on your own terms?

CHAPTER 7

Unlocking Your Gifts

Many people die with their music still in them.

OLIVER WENDELL HOLMES

The power in purpose means unlocking our gifts—those of which we're already aware and are motivated to master and those that are emerging that we would like to try or explore.

We each possess gifts and natural talents. This fundamental assumption has proved true for everyone whom I have coached over the past forty years. Everyone is gifted in some way. Many of us might deny that this is the case simply because we have focused on our weaknesses rather than our strengths.

Although talents are a part of everyday vocabulary, few people try to state clearly what their most naturally enjoyed gifts are. The power behind our purpose is knowing and using our most-enjoyed gifts. This chapter will help you answer these questions: What are my gifts? How can I best give my gifts to something in which I believe—a value, product, person, service, ideal, problem, or organization?

Everyone Is Gifted

We all have natural abilities and inclinations and find that certain things come easily to us. We may perform a talent so effortlessly that we forget we have it. This is a gift. We might not have had to pay the price to invest in this gift because it came so easily; we might have been born with it! We may never even have had to practice it extensively.

Our upbringing has convinced many of us that anything requiring hard work is valuable, and anything that comes easily and does not require hard work is worthless. About our gifts we often think, "This comes easily, so it must be easy for everyone." We underestimate its worth. Actually, our enjoyed gifts are our most powerful talents of all. And to be fulfilled in our lives, we must unlock and express them.

Some researchers say that we have numerous talents and ways of experiencing our innate intelligence. The theory of multiple intelligences was proposed by Howard Gardner, a Harvard University educator, in 1983. In his book *Frames of Mind,* he reported on his initial studies, which concluded that people have at least seven possible intelligences. He recently added an eighth.[13] These categories are summarized below. As you read, consider how you see yourself fitting into these eight areas. Which areas represent your most-enjoyed gifts?

1. **Verbal-linguistic:** *to think in words; to use language to express and understand complex meanings.* Do you like word games, puns, rhymes, or tongue twisters?

Do you use words correctly and persuasively? If you are attracted to this area, then tasks that require language—reading, writing, and speaking—are your natural talents. You are able to write clearly and can instruct or communicate through the spoken word. Sample work you might enjoy and excel in: attorney, journalist, poet, public relations director.

2. **Logical-mathematical:** *to connect cause and effect; to understand relationships among actions, objects, or ideas.* Do you use numbers effectively? Do you like facts, figures, or balancing your checkbook? If you are attracted to this area, then numbers and logic—reasoning, critical thinking, and mathematical problem solving—are your natural talents. You are able to make sense of your world by taking a rational, logical approach. Sample work for you: accountant, scientist, computer programmer, electrical engineer.

3. **Visual-spatial:** *to think in pictures; to perceive the visual world accurately.* Do you think visually? Do you have a vivid imagination or perceive colors, textures, shapes, and relationships among shapes accurately? If you are attracted to this area, then thinking in images and using shapes and color to portray the world around you are your natural talents. You are able to visualize, draw, paint, or sketch your ideas and are easily oriented to three-dimensional spaces. Sample work: architect, pilot, artist, interior designer.

4. **Musical:** *to think in sounds, rhythms, melodies, and rhymes.* Do you like humming tunes, making them up, or singing along with the radio? Do you appreciate and understand musical composition? If you are attracted to this area, then rhythms and melodies—singing in tune, keeping time to rhythms, and having an ear for music—are your natural abilities. You are able to listen to and discern different selections of musical pieces and appreciate compositions of all kinds. Sample work: music teacher, choir director, songwriter, musician, vocalist.

5. **Kinesthetic:** *to use the body in skilled and complicated ways for expressive activities.* Do you like to exercise, play sports, dance, or work with your hands? Do you move your body effectively and gracefully? If you are attracted to this area, then manipulating objects, demonstrating athletic prowess, and hands-on problem solving are your natural abilities. You are able to assemble things, build models, sculpt, dance, and enjoy physical activities of all kinds. Sample work: actor, dancer, athlete, choreographer, outdoor guide.

6. **Interpersonal:** *to think about and understand another person.* Are you sensitive to the feelings of others? Do you form successful relationships with others and enjoy teamwork? If you are attracted to this area, then tuning into the needs, feelings and desires of others—understanding and working with others—are your natural abilities. You are able to

see the world from another's perspective and connect effectively with people in the world around
you. Sample work: nurse, teacher, counselor, coach,
physician, entrepreneur.

7. **Intrapersonal:** *to think about and understand oneself.* Do you like to meditate or ponder the impon-
derables? Do you enjoy solitude and reflection? If
you are attracted to this area, then being self-reflec-
tive—aware of your deep self, your inner feelings
and motivations—are your natural abilities. You
are able to spend time alone to reflect on the world
around you in an independent, self-disciplined, and
self-motivated way Sample work: clergy, psychologist, executive/leader, philosopher, artist.

8. **Naturalistic:** *to understand the natural world, including plants, animals, and scientific studies.* Do
you like to classify and analyze how things fit together? If you are attracted to this area, then sens-
ing, understanding, and systematically classifying
the natural world—the environment—are your
natural abilities. You have an intuitive sense of how
things fit together and are able to distinguish inter-
relationships in the world. Sample work: biologist,
farmer, veterinarian, meteorologist.

Looking at gifts with Gardner's framework expands
the possibilities for unlocking our gifts. This framework
enables us to place value on a broad range of abilities
and helps us see our differences as strengths.

Confirm Your Gifts

Early in life, we learn to feel that some talents are more valuable to society than others are. Thus, we often don't acknowledge our gifts because we say, How could I make a living doing that? or What economic value could that gift possibly have? Unlocking our gifts means overcoming the tendency to discredit our gifts as less worthy than others'. Instead, we accept that we each have valuable gifts.

Unlocking our gifts also means overcoming any arrogance that exaggerates our own gifts at the expense of the gifts of others. We can present our gifts without self-display; we don't need to pretend to be what we are not. There is nothing for others to see through. There is no significant gap between how we act and what we really feel. Our gifts are self-evident. We can't help ourselves. Our hand turns naturally to that which we must enjoy.

If you're confused about what your gifts are, you can ask your spouse, a friend, a colleague, a supervisor, or someone who knows you very well to help you clarify and focus on your gifts.

If you wish to spend the time and energy to unlock or confirm your gifts in depth, you might consider doing the Calling Cards Exercise offered by Inventure—The Purpose Company (www.richardleider.com)[14] and Life Reimagined, LLC (www.lifereimagined.org).

We Do Best What We Enjoy Most

The idea that we should find fulfillment in our work is one that many people feel ambivalent about, both

accepting and questioning. Yet it seems to make sense
that we do best what we enjoy most, and when we use
our gifts, we find our work fulfilling.

There's a general notion that work is something
to be tolerated and leisure is something to be enjoyed.
Yet work consumes the most significant number of our
waking hours. When we consider that we spend about
60 percent of our life's time working, common sense
suggests that we discover work that is fulfilling. We can
refuse to go to our graves with our music still inside us.

Our work takes up the largest chunk of our waking
hours each week. To a large degree, it determines our
quality of life, depending on the location of the work
and the amount of money earned. Where we live, who
we become friends with, and what opportunities come
our way are influenced by the work we do and where
we do it.

When our work is not aligned with what we need
and enjoy in basic ways, problems in other areas of our
life are affected. The mental and physical costs of personal frustration and stress can be high.

Thus, knowing ourselves—what we do well and enjoy doing—is important not only for making work and
volunteer choices but also for living more fulfilling lives.
As you think about your present work or volunteer activities, ask yourself, Is this a good match for my most
enjoyed gifts? As you consider new work or volunteer
activities, ask, Is this likely to be a good match for my
most enjoyed gifts?

CHAPTER 8

Unlocking Your Curiosity

～

*This is the true joy in life, the being used for a purpose
recognized by yourself as a mighty one; the being thoroughly worn out before you are thrown on the scrap heap;
the being a force of Nature instead of a feverish selfish
little clod of ailments and grievances complaining that
the world will not devote itself to making you happy.*

GEORGE BERNARD SHAW

What's Worth Doing?

Now that you have considered your gifts, where do you
express them? For the sake of what? An important next
step is to unlock your curiosity and find out what moves
you. This is the hard part for many of us because we
believe the old adage, "Anything worth doing is worth
doing well." Most of the emphasis—mistakenly, I believe—has been put on the "worth doing well." The
real question is, "What's worth doing?"—a much-ne-
glected question for many of us. What issues, interests,
causes, or curiosities capture your genuine enthusiasm?
What keeps you up at night?

In the answers to questions like these, we can unlock our passions. Our passions, simply stated, are our

curiosities—those things we care most deeply about. Whatever form they take, passions are identified by their vitality. They are "alive" and we feel them deeply. A passion moves us to action in the world. Moreover, a passion doesn't quit but keeps recurring in our thinking and experiences.

When you have a good idea of what your gifts are and what moves you, you will have two of the three key ingredients of the power of purpose (the third is your values, discussed in the last chapter). Life and work choices based on gifts, passions, and value produces a purposeful life. The answer to the question, What's worth doing? will be different for each of us. This chapter will help you answer the question for yourself to help unlock your curiosity.

"Someone Oughta Do Something!"

When I wrote the first edition of this book, I worked at a small antique desk in my hundred-year-old, hand-hewn cabin built by immigrants—people who were new to this country—in the north woods of Wisconsin. I was surrounded by books on the topic, so absorbed in my task I sometimes felt I was in an altered state of consciousness. I often lost track of time as idea after idea popped into my mind from some deep well of curiosity. According to Mihalyi Csikszentmihalyi, distinguished professor of psychology at Claremont Graduate University, I was in "flow"—so curious about my topic that I lost touch with time.

In his book *Flow: The Psychology of Optimal Experience,* Csikszentmihalyi states his belief that we come closest to total fulfillment when in the flow state. He has concluded from his research that a passionate drive to solve problems and meet challenges causes us to derive pleasure from performing the task itself. By losing ourselves in our passions, we lose ourselves in time.

To consider potential opportunities where we can plug in our gifts, we must "tap into the flow state"[15] to think of what needs move us in our work, our organization, our family, our community, or society in general, and then examine those problems, issues, or concerns we feel curious about. What are the needs of your family, neighborhood, community, business, spiritual organization, the world? What needs doing? What issues do you truly feel "someone oughta do something about?"

Curiosity Questions

To stimulate your curiosity thinking, ask yourself these questions:

- If you were asked to create a TV special about something that moves you, what would it be about?

- What magazines intrigue you most at a newsstand? What sections or articles capture your attention?

- If you started a business or organization in order to solve a need, what would it be?

- What issue would you like to write (or read) a best-selling book about?

- What subjects are you curious to learn about? Go back to school for? Study under a master in?

- In the past year, what cause did you contribute time or money to? What interests does it reflect?

- Who are the people you find yourself voluntarily getting together with, again and again, for deeper discussions? What are your deepest conversations obsessing about?

- How would you use a gift of a million dollars if it had to be given away or designated for a cause, is-sue, or problem that moves you? What business or venture would you start?

- Is there any need or problem you believe in so strongly you'd love to work at it full time if you were paid to do it?

There is an old East African Swahili saying: *kuisi kwingi, koura mengi*. Roughly translated, it means that when you live a long life, you see and learn a lot. For me, the truth of this saying is powerful and profound. During the writing of this new edition, I spent time thinking about this saying and what I have learned since I wrote the first edition. One key learning is about how curiosity often drives purpose. If you're having a hard time grasping a sense of purpose, focus on your curios-ity. It will often help you to unlock your purpose!

The Power of Curiosity

When I turned sixty-five, my Medicare card arrived,

triggering a new curiosity about positive aging. Today, we "seasoned citizens," who represent one of the largest demographic segments in the United States, have a serious curiosity for learning. In fact, research points to curiosity as one of the key ingredients in longevity.

My own curiosity about aging began when I was in fifth grade. My church youth group volunteered at a local nursing home to cheer up the folks by reading and singing. The odors, the wheelchairs—coupled with the piercing moans and yells of a few residents—stayed with me for a long time. In fact, it wasn't until I reached age twenty-nine and received a Bush Foundation Fellowship to study positive aging that my perspective on aging shifted from negative to positive aging.

And now, at age seventy-one, it is shifting again. I have seen and learned a lot, and I love being this age and working with people of a "certain age" who have curiosity. Nothing is worse, for me, than being stuck on an airplane or at a dinner party next to a "former" anything—former executive, former teacher, former scientist—someone who is stuck in their former life. My strong preference is to sit next to someone who has a powerful curiosity about just about anything!

Walking the Great Wall in China, looking at the moon through a powerful telescope, saving a wild and scenic ruin, building a home with Habitat for Humanity, becoming a mentor for Big Brothers/Big Sisters. What do these have in common? They all evidence the power of curiosity.

In my coaching work, I encounter people who seem driven by something outside themselves, whose passion for their work or volunteer activities, their community, or their cause seems to rise above the possible. Indeed, we say that in such people we see the power of purpose. I sense that their lives are guided by a powerful curiosity—something more important than simple survival, but not merely intellectual—something in their souls. It's beyond our power as human beings to look into the souls of our fellow human beings to measure their power of hope or curiosity. Our best possibility for understanding, let alone replicating, this inner fire that contributes so greatly to the world is to study their present passions, their stories, the longing look in their eyes, and the joy they want to bring to those around them.

"What Are You Good At? How Can You Help?"

Neil Lovell and Jane Caldwell are two such people whom I met in London. Both work for the nonprofit charity, Kids Company. Kids Company was founded by Camila Bat-Manghelidjh to provide practical, emotional and educational support to vulnerable children and young people from the most deprived areas of London. Camila's deep passion to create a best-practice model of care to be replicated nationwide prompted Neil and Jane to take a major leap and join the Kids Company movement. I never met Camila, but her purpose was a palpable presence in the room.

Before joining Kids Company, Jane had established three companies in which she was the creative director. She also had worked as an independent film producer making documentaries and feature films, including the multiple-award-winning film *Foreign Moon,* directed by Zhang Zeming. She produced music promos for Sony and has written and directed plays for the theater. So why would she leave all this behind to join Kids Company? Jane sums it up in one word: "passion." She now directs the hugely successful arts program, encompassing visual arts, fashion, music, drama, and dance.

"The majority of those kids who seek our help suffer from severe emotional and behavioral difficulties resulting from significant experiences of trauma and neglect," Jane explains. "Many are 'lone children' living in chronic deprivation, with limited or no support from the adults in their life. I can relate to this in my own life experience."

Neil came to Kids Company with more than twenty-two years of broad communications, marketing, and business experience in agencies and in-house roles for big organizations. "Most of the organizations I have worked in have undergone significant change, including rebranding and mergers and acquisitions communications," relates Neil. "Over time," he says, "it wore me down. I needed to rekindle the flame."

Now Neil directs fund-raising and external relations at Kids Company, and he sums up his new feeling toward work as "passion." He says, "Kids Company's aim is to promote and support emotional well-being. Our approach is rooted in attachment theory, which I am deeply curious about. We are pioneering in the areas of child abuse, neglect, and trauma, and have received support and recognition from the government to replicate our work in other areas."

Neil and Jane both experienced purpose moments upon meeting Camila. She asks only two questions: "What are you good at?" and "How can you help?" In answering these questions, Neil said, "My story suddenly made sense, what I was here to do. Finally I could see how it all fit together—how my life up to this point had, in fact, prepared me to meet Camila." Jane realized, "A lot of money didn't really do it for me. I yearned for a cause, a passion to guide my work. Camila modeled that and I wanted it, too."

Jane and Neil, along with others, are helping to lead Kids Company to the next level of effectiveness by bringing their gifts and passions, plus experiences from their past work lives, to create the future for Kids Company. In doing so, they are also creating a more meaningful future for themselves.

With age and life experience can come a feeling of freedom and liberation to pursue our passions. We are now, hopefully, more mature. We have gained practical wisdom about what's worth doing with our time, talents, and money. Our value systems have shifted away from self-absorption toward generativity—giving back to life. For people like Jane and Neil, passion is a powerful thing. They were willing to take big risks on things they care about.

Bringing Life and Livelihood Together

Theologian Matthew Fox writes, "A spirituality of work is about bringing life and livelihood back together again. And spirit with them." He claims, "Spirit means life, and both life and livelihood are about living in depth, living with meaning, purpose, joy, and a sense of contributing to the greater community."[16]

Sally Humphries Leider, my spouse and purpose partner, brings "life and livelihood" together. And spirit with them. She says, "I always felt natural doing what I was doing. I love to teach children, to bring out their essence, their spirit." Throughout her life, Sally has immediately connected with children as her natural learning partners. Ever since she was in the third grade, Sally was in awe of teachers. She says, "My fantasy was to be able to sit on the ground outdoors with my second-grade teacher and just talk."

When Sally started her teaching career in the city, she missed the out-of-doors most of all. Having grown up on a river in natural surroundings, she says, "I was given the gift of place—the gift of growing up in a place which was rich with the sounds, sights, and smells of nature. I took place for granted until my parents died and I couldn't go back to the river anymore." She tried to find the same feeling in other places but couldn't find it. So, she moved back to the river—a place she loves and is passionate to preserve.

Sally's parents were active in support of the environment, willing to fight, lobby, and educate people about preserving the natural river valley they lived in. Sally carries on their battle. Today, as a professional watershed educator, activist, and life coach, Sally says her purpose is "to instill a sense of place in people of all ages." She feels a legacy to continue the hard work her parents left her of maintaining the natural harmony in nature. Through her Watershed Wisdom classes at the local schools, and her Wild Indigo coaching practice with young women in transition, she inspires young people to develop a deep sense of place. Her parents gave her the place, growing up, to love nature and notice things in nature. They taught her what's worth saving and preserving and working for.

Sally's deep passion is eco-literacy—the importance of place-based education as fundamental to educating for sustainability. She believes in the intrinsic value of all nature, rather than the idea that the natural environment is a resource for human exploitation. She believes that "biodiversity, the total variety of life on earth, is collapsing at mind-boggling rates. The accelerating loss of plant and animal species is occurring all over the planet."

To stop the losses, Sally believes that a critical aspect of awareness for all of us is to experience nature directly. She says, "To the extent that we can discover for ourselves a special connection with the natural world, we will be potentially motivated to take action to preserve the earth's species and ecosystems. That's my purpose, to give people that experience."

At the end of *Flow*, Csikszentmihalyi offers a prescription for the power of purpose. He says we can transform our whole life into a unified flow experience by approaching our activities in a certain way, by pursuing what he calls a "life theme." Whatever our passion, "as long as it provides clear objectives, clear rules for action, and a way to concentrate and become involved, any goal can serve to give meaning to a person's life." Sally has a reason to get up in the morning—to pursue her "life theme."

Can you detect a life theme in your activities? Are you pursuing it?

PART III

Purpose and Work

CHAPTER 9

The 24-Hour Purpose Retreat

೧

We have not come into the world to be numbered;
we have been created for a purpose;
for great things: to love and be loved.

MOTHER TERESA OF CALCUTTA

There is no better way to unlock the power of purpose than taking a day away from your usual schedule to reflect on what truly matters to you.

Everyone can live purposefully for one day. The person who unlocks their purpose makes that day the pattern for every day!

People who have done a purpose retreat often share that they were surprised how just twenty-four hours of "solo time" to reflect on their lives affected them at a deep level and helped them make sense of things. Some even decided to make it an annual ritual to reimagine their lives at home and work.

This chapter serves as your retreat guide for reflecting on the life you want to lead. What follows are the questions designed to help you write a purpose statement. Use these questions to guide you through your own reflective experience. By the end of your retreat, you won't have any hesitation in answering the question, "Why do I get up in the morning?"

Solo Time

Your purpose retreat is personal. It is important that you spend the time alone.

Start by deciding to go somewhere alone—a quiet place where you can go "solo" for about twenty-four hours. It may be a nature setting or just a special place where you are comfortable and won't be distracted by television, mobile phone, email, surfing the internet, or other people.

Plan ahead for hydration, food, and shoes comfortable enough to take a walk in. Fresh air and periodic short walks will help inspire your thought process. During your retreat, figure out a rhythm that keeps you focused.

Write your insights in a purpose journal, or use your laptop and follow the questions suggested. Write whatever comes to mind. Sometimes our first thoughts become our best thoughts. Allow your imagination to take you places outside your comfort zone. Let go of negative assessments and doubts until later. You might recall experiences from your past you thought were over or complete. Those recollections might, now, take on new meaning.

Let's Begin

Once you arrive at your "solo site," unpack and settle into your space. Get going. Take three deep breaths until you're feeling centered. Do this often during your twenty-four hours.

Preview the questions that follow. The questions are straightforward, designed to build on one another. If you get stuck on a question, feel free to put the question aside and return to it later. Take a walk to reflect on the question. But, be sure to answer all the questions from start to finish.

Before you begin, read the following overview.

What's It All About?

A sense of life purpose promotes physical, mental, and spiritual health. Purpose is fundamental.

People who seek meaning beyond themselves are healthier, happier, and live longer. So, it's vital to our well-being that we maintain a strong sense of purpose.

For some people, life purpose is a spiritual concept, or has a religious dimension. For others, it's a more secular notion, a need to be valued as a member of a family or group.

Not everyone feels comfortable writing a purpose statement, but we all need one.

As we mature through the phases of our life, experiencing various levels of psychological, emotional, and ultimately, spiritual growth, we might come to think more deeply about our life purpose and find ourselves yearning for deeper levels of meaning.

At some phase of our lives, we might feel stuck, going nowhere, drifting without direction, wondering "what's it all about?"

Here are seven ways to unlock your purpose and answer that question.

Seven Questions to Unlock Purpose

There are no rigid formulas for how to reflect about purpose, but there are many helpful techniques to assist you. Here are seven mind-changing ideas that have brought powerful results to many people over the years. Use them to see what you can discover about yourself.

1. Think about this sentence for a moment: "From family and friends who knew me when I was very young, I have heard that my 'special gift' is _____." How have these "gifts" persisted in your life?

2. Imagine being on your deathbed, still clear and coherent, when your best friend drops in to visit you. Your friend asks, "Did you give and receive love?" "Were you authentically you?" "Did you make a small difference in the world?" How did you answer the questions?

3. Get out a calculator and do some "life math." Multiply your age × 365 (____). Then, subtract that number from 30,000 (____), an average life expectancy. Once you get clear that you have (____) more times to wake up, it might inspire you to live more courageously now. How do you feel about how you are spending your most precious currency—your time?

4. What mood do you wake up with most mornings? Do you resist getting up or do you get out of

bed with energy and purpose? Think about the way you wake up, these days, and you will learn something about your life's purpose.

5. After the retreat, write the question, "What are my gifts?" on five index cards. Give them to five people who know you well and ask them to write their response to the question on the card. Put them all together in a place where you can see them. Who are the five people that you will select? What theme or thread do you anticipate that you will discover?

6. Curious? What are you most curious about? Here are some clues that will help you answer:

    a. Time passes quickly when you're spending time on this.

    b. It's so natural you can't help spending time on it!

    c. You enjoy it so much, your worries disappear when you're thinking about it or experiencing it.

    d. A bad day doing this is better than a good day doing most other things.

7. Who are your models and mentors? Ask yourself who is really leading the kind of life and doing the kind of work that you envision in the next phase of your life? After the retreat, initiate a courageous conversation to find out more about them.

Use these seven questions to inform your "writing my purpose statement" exercise.

Reflect on the Big Question

Push the "pause button" on your writing and reflect for a moment on this question: "Are we born with purpose, or do we choose one?"

If you ask enough people, you'll probably find that there are two basic schools of thought regarding life purpose:

- Those who believe that a life purpose is something that we are born with, that it is planted in our souls before we are born and we must embody or achieve it. It's our embedded destiny, so to speak, and we have no choice in the matter.

- Those who believe that fate and destiny don't exist and we have the power (or free will) to choose our life purpose and do what we choose with our lives.

Which group do you belong to? Destiny? Or, choice?

There are no easy or perfect answers to this question. So, if you're still not sure, consider this workable compromise. What if a life purpose is something you are born with, but you also have full control over how and when you activate it? What if, with a little reflection and choice, you could move naturally and easily toward your life purpose without feeling like you "have to" do specific things?

You might be surprised to discover that unlocking your life purpose can be an enjoyable process. It's the kind of choice that changes everything—from emptiness to fulfillment, from boredom to passion. Humans were created for choice.

Choice Is the Power in Purpose

Consider choosing a new mindset—that of "living purposefully" rather than "having a purpose."

Living purposefully means choosing how you will use your gifts and talents to create more meaning for yourself and others.

When it comes to living purposefully, we usually find ourselves in one of three places:

- We don't worry about whether we have a formal purpose or not. We simply live our lives doing the things we feel drawn to.

- We know exactly what our purpose is, and we live it each day.

- We believe we have a purpose but are challenged by what it may be or how to find out.

Which group do you fall into?

Members of the first group probably wouldn't be doing a purpose retreat, and members of the second group would probably be too busy living purposefully to reflect about it!

The majority of people who go on a retreat probably fall into group number three. If you're not sure if you do, reflect further on these questions:

Have you recently felt like you'd like to be doing more with your life?

- Do you often yearn to use your gifts (natural talents) to contribute more to the world?

- Do you feel like you're "majoring in the minors"—wasting time on things that are too small for you?

- Do you desire to "major in the majors"—serve others in a larger way but don't know how?

- Do you ever wonder "is this all there is?"

If you answered "yes" to these questions, you're probably ready to write your purpose statement.

Your "Default Purpose"

In simple terms, our "default purpose" is to GROW and to GIVE!

In no sense is any life purposeless. How do we know this?

Let's begin at the beginning. From the standpoint of evolutionary biology, the ultimate purpose of life is to sustain life. To "sustain life" means much more than just to survive and reproduce. Survival requires constant growth.

Nature doesn't stand still; Change is the only constant. This is a fundamental law we can't avoid. To change is to either "grow or survive" or "decay and die."

We humans don't just grow physically. We also experience "inner growth." We grow intellectually, emotionally, spiritually, and socially.

Community connection is vital for survival. The needs to grow and give are essential elements to our evolutionary survival strategy (along with intelligence and choice). Our early ancestors learned the wisdom, in survival terms, of personal growth, and of giving today because they might need help tomorrow.

Our Growth Determines Our Capacity to Give

Through our inner growth as individuals, we collectively contribute to the advancement of the community as a whole. The greater our individual growth, the greater the clarity of our gifts serving those around us. Through them in turn, our impact extends indefinitely, ever rippling outwards. The quality and individual reach of our service to others is what differs. We give to our family, community, and world in accordance with the quality of growth we project.

As we grow, this impact becomes more subtle, refined, and more powerful. The power of purpose.

Inner "growth," then, is essential to our outer "giving."

The gifts we give will be framed and scaled by the phase of our life, and by our present roles, responsibilities, and maturity. We may, for example, be a parent, a business person, a teacher, a student, a caregiver, an employee, a retired person, or be in any number of these or other roles. Each of our phases and roles in life carries choices for us to grow and to give.

Our life purpose involves a quest for growth and a search for meaning through giving. Our purpose evolves as we grow through life phases. Purpose grows and develops with us.

Purpose Is Intention

So, your default purpose is to "Grow and to Give!"

The dictionary defines purpose as: An object or result aimed at: Intention

What does this suggest? A purpose can be as simple as your intention or a direction. So, a "life purpose" statement is really nothing more (or less) than your intention to live in a certain direction.

A life purpose is realized through intention by getting to know your authentic self, uncovering your gifts, and choosing the best possible expression to share them with the world.

Finding your purpose is a misleading concept because it's not something we have to go out and "get," but rather something we need to turn within and "unlock."

We've already got it—even if we haven't clarified it yet!

How do we unlock it? By looking in the most essential places—our gifts, passions, and values. Why would we be given a life purpose that doesn't match the true nature of who we are?

Before we can write our life purpose statement, we need to search for the clues that lead to it.

A Purpose Clue

Clue: What are my strongest beliefs?
Jot down your thoughts on the following:

Community: What do you think your responsibility is to others?

Service: What is life asking of you, today?

Values: What do you stand for?

Legacy: What do you think your life's legacy will be?

Wisdom: Who are the wise elders in your life? What was/is their advice?

Compassion: What do you think is its nature and importance?

Source: If you have a concept of God, Supreme Being, or Higher Power, what do you think the Source is expecting of you?

Writing Your Purpose Statement

Using your beliefs as clues, draft a purpose statement. If you find it easier, jot down a number of statements to see how they look and feel to you.

The reason I get up in the morning is to: awaken, ignite, organize, teach, support, empower, develop, accept, encourage, help, inspire, earn, enhance, serve, lead, act upon, ...

Examples: "I get up in the morning to bring out the best in my colleagues." "I get up in the morning to help people become as much as they can be." "I get up in the morning to make the world a little greener and kinder."

Write a single draft phrase, which expresses your reason for getting up in the morning.

I get up in the morning to _____

_____.

Writing a purpose statement is challenging. If you find it difficult to write your purpose statement, don't be discouraged. View it as a question, "What gets me up in the morning?" Live in the question every morning for the next week after the retreat. Don't be put off by the work of writing the statement. There's nothing mystical or mysterious about it. Yet, it does require some work. It's rarely revealed to us without some digging.

The search for life purpose is far more straightforward than we might expect. Getting it wrong, over and over, is part of the process. It's how we grow.

One-Week "Default Purpose"

First thing each morning for one week, ask yourself, How will I grow and give, today? At the end of each day, reflect on what "meaning moments" made you feel as if you were growing and giving.

CHAPTER 10

Working with Presence

༄

*This book is about a search, too, for daily meaning as well
as daily bread, for recognition as well as cash, for aston-
ishment rather than torpor; in short, for a sort of life
rather than a Monday through Friday sort of dying.*

STUDS TERKEL

Daily Bread and Daily Meaning

Earlier in human history, people offered their daily activities as a thank you to God, because all enterprise was
ultimately intended for God. This was the basis for the
infamous work ethic, with which many people have an
ambivalent relationship. However, the concept of stewardship, by which one made an offering to God of one's
best efforts, elevated a person's work to the status of a
calling.

A calling comes from the inside out; it is the expression of our presence. Our calling is an expression of the
spirit at work in the world through us. It is that mysterious voice that calls us to find our voice and to play our
music. A calling means bringing presence to work. A
calling calls forth the deeper questions of work, such as
how, why, and for whom we do our work.

Once you have some understanding of your gifts and have identified your passion, the third key ingredient that powers your purpose is your calling. A calling adds the value of service to passion and gifts. Every individual is by creation essentially a servant. And this is possible because each of us has been born with certain unique gifts to serve others.

So now we face the question: Is work a job—daily bread alone. Or can work be synonymous with a calling—daily bread and daily meaning? This chapter will help you explore the idea of calling and what it takes to find meaning in your work.

Worked or Working?

My coaching work involves helping people become clearer about the presence or absence of a calling in their work. Since I became passionate about the importance and benefits of the call in work, I have made a practice of interviewing people I meet who seem "called to" their work. This helps to test my hypothesis that the strongest motivations are associated with a connection to some higher purpose or calling.

Of course, many people who report to work every day are cynical and burned-out; they have given up and seem content to make it to quitting time. Many people genuinely feel overworked. In the words of the German mystic Meister Eckhart, they are "worked" instead of working. Many believe it is ethically important for them to work hard, though they don't see any larger common good deriving from their work.

However, the people who perform most energetically, creatively, and enthusiastically are those who believe they are contributing to a mission, purpose, or cause outside of and larger than themselves. The failure of many organizations to enlist people in some kind of larger, non-quantitative mission is at the root of many motivation problems today. When we ignore purpose at work, we inhibit our highest motivator.

Finding and heeding a call—a work mission that goes beyond ourselves—has many naturally productive consequences. It provides us with a source of deep presence. We are clear about how others may benefit from our efforts. A call provides an aim for our conduct and a focus for being more fully present at work.

The notion of heeding the call may take a while to digest. It requires an openness of the heart and—above all—presence. The discovery of our calling often requires an incubation period. The architect Le Corbusier said that the birth of a project was just like the birth of a child: "There's a long period of gestation ... a lot of work in the subconscious before I make the first sketch. That lasts for months. One fine morning the project has taken form without my knowing it." The "birth" of one's calling may feel like this.

Most of us want to feel that we are significant and that our work calls us to something enduring and worthwhile. More than anything else, naturally productive work enables us to spend our precious time in ways that express our gifts, passions, and values.

Can Purpose Keep You Alive?

I meet many people today who feel called. We're all called. Few of us choose to answer the call.

The lives of people who follow their calling are fascinating. They are read about, talked about, and sometimes used as models for living a life that matters. Their lives invite questions of why they were chosen and how they recognized their calling.

Dan Petersen nearly died. He chose to live. While recovering from cancer surgery, his heart went out of control. Not once, but twice. He was shocked back to life. He vividly recalls, "After I awakened and was being transported on a gurney to monitored care, I was left in an alcove awaiting a room. I was sure that I was dying. My focus was only on my breathing. And, gratitude. I was flooded with gratitude, not only for surviving, but for the gift of life itself."

Since facing death, and surviving, Dan's life has shifted. Out of that sense of gratitude has emerged a deepened sense of calling.

A deeper calling consciously started for Dan when he completed his studies to become an orthodontist. Looking back, Dan says, "I was operating with an undeclared purpose to set my life up with enough money and enough time to follow my longing for adventure. I wanted to work half of the year and be adventurous with the other half."

And Dan did just that for twenty-two years. At that point, he left a successful private practice to follow his calling to study holistic healing. He recalls, "Something very powerful was calling me; so powerful, I was willing to give up almost everything to discover it. It was in the form of a question: "How does self-healing occur?"

He left his practice to return to school to study his passion—the body-mind connection. He believed that self-healing systems function optimally when there's a higher consciousness—a higher sense of purpose.

Dan's purpose today is "to mediate the conditions for change." He has the same calling he had fifteen years ago but in a deeper form. As a life coach, he provides an environment in which the body, mind, emotions, and spirit can self-heal by mediating conditions for a deeper understanding of oneself and the world we live in.

Dan believes that the optimal environment for self-healing is "freedom of expression, meaningful purpose, compassion, and listening." So, he is talking less and listening more. After his near-death experience, he says, "I find that when people slow down enough and pay attention to the bigger picture, they can articulate what they long for and how that has too often moved to the back burner of a busy life."

Working with Presence

We find the call from inside ourselves. We sense that there is something unique and special that we can contribute and that the kind of life, work, or volunteer work we do should align with these contributions. Heeding the call starts when our "music"—an aim, a passion, an interest, a problem, an idea—attracts us enough to move us to action on its behalf. It is important enough so that focusing on it directs our activities and gives our lives meaning.

We all have had many opportunities—purpose moments—that could lead us to heed the call in our lives. The question we must ask ourselves is, Was I present when the opportunity presented itself? Heeding the call requires that we be present in our work, making choices that are aligned with what we care most about. Heeding the call also requires courage.

Are you ready to bring your whole self to work? Can you find the courage to be present and follow where it leads?

CHAPTER 11

The Working-on-Purpose Quiz

෮

Our chief usefulness to humanity rests on our combining power with higher purpose. Power undirected by high purpose spells calamity, and high purpose by itself is utterly useless if the power to put it into effect is lacking.

THEODORE ROOSEVELT

In my years as a life coach, I have seen many people who are reframing their definition of "success." Some people measure success in strictly financial terms. Others have a broader definition of success, but their vision is not consistent with the purpose of the organization for which they work. And judging by the dramatic rise in the number of stress-related problems among workers at all levels, many feel alienated from any meaning in their work.

This chapter will explore the meaning of success and provide a quiz to help you determine if your work aligns with it.

What Is Success?

Toward what success do we strive? The work ethic, for many of us, does not seem to be dead or even dying. For some of us, success is the advancement of our careers. We will make tremendous sacrifices for a career, will bend over backward to avoid making waves to advance it, and will treat ourselves as resumes to be packaged and marketed to further it. The consequence of such an orientation to success is that we become motivated primarily by personal gain—what our work will get us.

Yet when we look beneath the surface of such a drive for success, what's there? The result is a person with highly refined skills of the head, but not of the heart—a person who knows how to work but not how to be happy or satisfied or relaxed.

In *The Overworked American,* economist Juliet Schor describes "the squirrel cage of work and spend" that traps so many people. "Happiness," she claims, "has failed to keep pace with economic growth."[17] There is a false belief that the next purchase will yield happiness, or if not that one, then the next. But that belief merely sets us up for the squirrel-cage mentality of work, and spend, and work and spend some more. No matter how much we make, it is never enough. If we find no joy and meaning in the work we do, we will be stuck in this hopeless, unrewarding cycle.

However, there is another way. James Autry got it right when he wrote, "Work can provide the opportunity for spiritual and personal as well as financial growth. If it doesn't, we're wasting far too much of our lives on it."[18]

Modern society has given many of us the means to succeed financially and build apparently successful careers, but often we still cannot find fulfillment in our work. We find that if we strive for success as an end in itself, we rarely find it. And we are tired of working for organizations that consume us and offer money in return for stressful and unfulfilling work.

Further, in a restructured, shifting economy, many people are being forced to reconsider the merits of conventional success—such as security, advancement, and retirement. These disenfranchised and discouraged workers are beginning to place a higher value on work that has a deeper meaning, such as service, balance, community, and mission or purpose. They are asking: To what are we committed? Whom do we serve?

Finding Fulfilling Work

Many people argue against the practicality of finding fulfilling work. Rarely, however, does anyone argue against the desirability of such work.

The problem appears to be a gap between supply and demand of a most central thing—fulfilling work— work that fully engages our talents in something we believe in. Perhaps one reason is that we don't really expect work to give us much meaning. I have observed at least four separate levels of work expectations:

First level: It's just a job; any job is okay as long as the money is good and we can do our thing after work.

Second level: It's a permanent job. At this level, our work has to be regular; we need benefits, vacations, and security.

Third level: It's a profession or trade. Rather than thinking only of money and security, we want substance in our work. We want to grow our talents and be challenged. At this level, we are still profoundly concerned with money, but we are also attached to the profession, or work, itself.

Fourth level: It is a calling. At this level, we realize that work is related to money but that work is also a path to use our gifts to make a difference doing something we believe needs doing in this world. We begin to consider the meaning that work can bring and the opportunity it allows us to find fulfillment, yet, follow a calling yet still have a marketable, income-producing involvement in the world.

The first step to finding fulfilling work—or to fulfillment in your current work—is to determine what level you are now working on. The Working-on-Purpose Quiz can help.

The Working-on-Purpose Quiz

To find work that is a source of "daily meaning and daily bread" takes time and thoughtful analysis.

Take a few minutes to take the Working-on-Purpose Quiz in the Resources section of this book. What are the signs in your work that indicate, "Yes, my work is on purpose?" What are the signs that indicate, "No, my work isn't as purposeful as I might wish?" Check either yes or no according to how you feel about each question today.

The total number of yes responses on the quiz provides a general idea of your power of purpose at work. If you have many yes responses, you're probably finding fulfillment in your work. If you have many no responses, you probably lack a sense of fulfillment, and you might consider further clarifying your gifts, passions, and values. The time taken to identify elements of fulfilling work is well invested.

Finding Fulfilling Work

Many leaders are discovering the connection between fulfilling work and productivity. Warren Malkerson was vice president and general manager of a large sporting goods catalogue company. He had felt this connection through his whole life but didn't understand it until he was in a big job. As a senior leader, he relates, "I always got criticized for caring too much about people. I felt a struggle being on the 'soft side,' like the ugly duckling."

One day he realized he was, in fact, not the ugly duckling but a swan—that fulfilling work was not only worthwhile but also productive. Wherever he has worked, it has been said, "His people always seem to be the happier, more creative folks in the organization."

Warren believes there's a swan at the core of every one of us. His purpose is "to help others discover their swan—the core inside." He feels that every human is struggling to discover his or her true potential.

Warren views every person as a learner. He considers his leadership to be effective when his colleagues say,

"I've never worked so hard and learned so much. He makes me learn!" He pledges to people when he hires them that they'll always be able to answer yes to the question, "Was this one of your best learning experiences?"

Like one of his heroes, the late quality guru Edward Deming, Warren believes, "I don't have to convert everybody! I'm not a missionary. I'm not here to help those who don't want to be helped. But my purpose is to help those who want to learn on purpose!"

Leaders like Warren, who are committed to the growth of others, clearly see that fulfilling work can be productive and profitable.

For the Sake of What?

A primary role of leaders, like Warren, is to answer the question many followers are asking today: "Why should I follow you?" Today, great leaders understand that all change is self-change; we really can't compel people to do anything. We can only create an environment where they want to do things. They understand that real commitment and discretionary energy come through purpose.

As a coach to many leaders, I have been impressed with the hunger that great leaders have for some purpose higher than just personal career and financial success. They want to know clearly what they are leading for—for the sake of what?

We yearn today for leaders who are leading with a "purpose mindset." Purpose is something lived every day—it can be seen in what leaders do rather than what they say. It is embodied in the way a leader spends his or her time.

It is helpful to observe leaders who are "on purpose." They are usually easy to spot, and when you spot one you know it instantly. Purposeful leaders naturally attract others because they are clear about the "for the sake of what?" question. They simply have a "purpose mindset" and people feel valued in their presence. We don't always recall what they did or said, but we always remember how they made us feel.

One person who has that mindset is Walter Mondale. I have lived in the same neighborhood as "Fritz" for twenty years and have seen how he treats people. He is generous and genuine in his connections to each person he meets. He makes considerable effort to learn about you—what you're working on, what your hopes are. He gives his gifts generously to needy causes. He is also generous with his ideas, his advice, and his desire to serve. He embodies the best practices of purposeful leadership.

One of my former teachers, Dr. Usarabudh Arya, taught me this: "As the flower unfolds, the bees come uninvited." That's Walter Mondale. His life is a testament to the wisdom of Dr. Arya. How many former U.S. vice presidents have devoted their lives to helping others fulfill their lives? And how many of them are eighty-seven years old and still serving? His flower continues to unfold and the bees continue to come uninvited.

Look for purpose moments right now. Many people delay, saying that one day—when they are retired or more secure—they will give back with their time, talent, or treasure. But the feeling of security cannot be obtained by accumulating more wealth. Being generative, in fact, actually makes people feel richer and less in need of more wealth. It also makes them feel less dependent on their wealth for security. That is why we need to start being generative now, or we might never experience the joy of generosity.

When we operate out of a spirit of generosity, we are enhanced spiritually and emotionally. And these benefits to spiritual and emotional well-being keep paying off because generosity changes us in positive ways. We like ourselves more, which causes others to respond more positively to us.

Is your work fulfilling? What is success to you, today?

PART IV

Purpose and Well-Being

CHAPTER 12

The School-of-Life Purpose

*Strange is our situation here upon earth. Each
of us comes for a short visit, not knowing why,
yet sometimes seeming to divine purpose. From the
stand point of daily life, however, there is one thing
we do know: that we are here for the sake of others...*

ALBERT EINSTEIN

Where do we go for an advanced degree in maturity?
Where do we get the life skills needed to live a purposeful life?

Being on purpose is a life skill. It is a way of living in
which you are here for the sake of others. Every situation presents you with a new purpose moment—an opportunity to show up on purpose—and you are aware
of your moment-to-moment choices.

In other words, living purposefully simply means
becoming aware of who you are and the choices you
are bringing to life during each day.

A good place to start living on purpose is to ponder the ultimate purpose question: Why? Why do I get
up in the morning? For many of us, this question is as
tough as it is inevitable. Ideally, we should not let too

many years pass without spending some time pondering the question. But, where do we go to ponder? Where do we go for an advanced degree in maturity?

This chapter will help you ponder the question and make the link between purpose and well-being.

What Is the School-of-Life Purpose?

The School-of-Life Purpose is called such because it is dedicated to exploring, well, purpose! It is dedicated to teaching the life skills to impact your well-being—your relationships, your work, your health, and your happiness.

Why?

Often we are so busy trying to answer the questions that we fail to take time to acknowledge, even celebrate, the "why?" questions. We believe meaning comes from quick answers. We can so easily sit down at the computer and Google the answers that we rarely take the time to push the pause button and live in the "why?" questions, the big questions that matter. Technology has accelerated life, we are in a hurry, and we have lost respect for the wisdom embodied in the questions themselves.

In 1907, the German poet Rainer Maria Rilke wrote a letter to a young poet advising:

> I would like to beg you, dear Sir, as well as
> I can, to have patience with everything un-
> resolved in your heart and to try to love the
> questions themselves as if they were locked
> rooms or books written in a very foreign

language. Don't search for the answers, which could not be given to you now, because you would not be able to live them. And the point is to live everything.[19]

First we need to pause and ask ourselves what we need in our lives. A need is something we must have to survive. After we are clear about our basic needs, we can begin to look at our wants. Wants enrich the quality of our lives. And what we truly want often reflects our purpose.

Maslow's Theory Revisited

Psychologist Abraham Maslow arranged human needs into a hierarchy.[20] He claimed that our basic needs must be at least minimally fulfilled before we can move toward our wants. Our physical needs (for example, air, food, shelter) are the most basic. These needs must be satisfied before we can free our energies to pursue needs at the next level. As Gandhi said, "Even God cannot talk to a hungry man except in terms of bread."

At the next level, according to Maslow, we must feel minimally safe and secure in our day-to-day activities. We all define safety and security in different ways, but the need to feel that our life and our work are rooted in solid ground is fundamental.

At the next level, we must feel a sense of companionship and affection. We need love—some kind of recognition that we have worth, that someone cares. Our self-worth can be badly damaged by the lack of real love. Self-worth will rise if we engage in life and work activities that we believe are worthwhile, in which we can be contributing members of society. To the extent that we spend our precious time on activities that we don't value, that we consider "worthless," our self-worth will diminish.

At the next level, we need to self-actualize. At this level we are growing, stretching, and utilizing our gifts and talents. Maslow wrote, "Even if all these needs are satisfied, we may still often (if not always) expect that a new discontent and restlessness will soon develop unless the individual is doing what he is fitted for. A musician must make music, an artist must paint, a writer must write if he is to be ultimately at peace with himself. What a [person] can be, [he or she] must be. This need we call self-actualization."

Maslow's thinking shifted beyond self-actualization over the course of his life. The shift occurred for two reasons: his conversations with Viktor Frankl and, his continuing study of "peak experiences"—mystical, aesthetic, and emotional experiences often involving nature. He came to recognize that the purpose of life is not to realize oneself, which he had termed self-actualization; rather, the purpose of life is to transcend oneself by giving to others.

He named this new motivational level "self-transcendence" to account for people, like Frankl, who were clearly self-actualized but also held an apparent desire to identify with something greater than themselves through service to others. By renaming self-transcendence as the new peak of his motivational pyramid, Maslow identified what powers purpose.

Where do you locate yourself on Maslow's Pyramid?

Four School-of-Life Purpose Lessons

Lesson 1: Avoid Inner Kill—the Death of Purpose!

A frequent complaint I hear in my coaching practice is a lack of fulfillment. Viktor Frankl called the feeling of emptiness, meaninglessness, or purposelessness the "existential vacuum." Such a state often results from the lack of fulfilling something larger than and outside of ourselves.

The existential vacuum is an attitude toward life held by too many people today. Take, for example, the vice president of a high-technology company whom I coach. "I just can't seem to get going," he said. "I used to be an up-and-coming executive with this company. Now I can't get interested in what I'm supposed to do. I know I should get rolling. I'm sleepwalking through the day. And I'm awake at night. I'm going to the liquor store twice a week when once used to be enough. I feel stuck!"

In short, he was struggling with the vacuum—with inner kill—the art of dying without knowing it! He felt stuck in a kind of vocational quicksand. He was not challenged. He felt he could not leave, nor could he stay.

He went on to say, "I don't know how much longer I can last in this job. I've been with the company for fifteen years and have changed jobs every two to three years. The organization charts keep changing, but the politics don't. We're still being told what we must do and when. The old virtues of initiative and taking risks are not being rewarded. The process of getting rewards is more political now. I'm dying."

What was happening to this executive? He felt that no one cared about the contribution he was making. That caused him to raise the question, Why do I get up in the morning? He'd lost sight of his purpose for working.

Most people experience inner kill at some point in their lives. If a person is not challenged by meaningful tasks and is spared the positive stress surrounding such tasks, inner kill occurs. It is the condition of dying from the inside out.

Inner kill is similar to a garden in which nothing grows—it's dead. Inner kill is the death of purpose. Life lacks purpose; nothing moves us. Our life lacks promise; it continues day after day at the same petty pace. Helen Keller said, "Life is either a daring adventure or nothing." That nothing is inner kill.

Like the more generalized depression, inner kill cuts across all ages and levels. People in these situations feel chronic fatigue, self-criticism, and anger or indifference. They can no longer invest themselves in others or in their work. Most of us recognize the phenomenon of being more or less awake on different days. With inner kill, our talents are slumbering.

Once people reach the point of inner kill, they often find it difficult to see any other possibilities for themselves. They are stuck in the drain of indecision.

Action: If you're feeling a sense of inner kill, discuss it with a committed listener—someone who practices care-vs-cure and who cares enough to listen without trying to fix you. Be totally transparent with how you feel.

Lesson 2: Avoid The Drain of Indecision!

Almost every person at some point in their life ponders, What's next? During each phase of our lives, we reflect on where we've been, where we're going, what we've accomplished, and what is possible. We wonder whether to stay or leave a job, hang onto or let go of a relationship. At times we may feel like we've become fugitives from ourselves. We yearn for ways to overcome the drain of indecision and find opportunities to reclaim our lives.

Some people are experiencing the pressures of life transitions and feel pulled in many directions—sandwiched between taking care of their children and their parents, dealing with divorce, remarriage, second families, blended families, empty nesting, widowhood, illness and recovery, and the list goes on.

At work, too, many people have reached a plateau and realize that their gifts are not being fully used. They feel that they have outgrown their jobs, companies, or even their fields. Some feel bored. Others feel blocked by leaders who they feel simply don't understand them. One or a combination of these feelings can make a person dislike getting up to go to work.

Millions of people are stuck in the drain of indecision, struggling alone with What's next? And how to get there. We feel stuck in the indecision cycle. To reclaim our lives, we must not avoid making decisions—we must express our inner selves in the outer world.

Action: Start where you are. Take this small step to explore "What's next?" Select a "sounding board" of three to five people with whom you can brainstorm. For 140 minutes, explore your dilemma. The focus is entirely on you.

Lesson 3: Avoid Avoiding the "What's It All About?" Question

What's it all about is not so much a single question but a placeholder for a whole set of questions: Why am I here? What am I meant to do? Is my life serving some greater purpose? Am I here to help others or just myself?

It occurred to psychologist Fred Kiel that he was losing his passion for his work. He was beginning to question why he was getting up and going to work in the morning. He was also questioning his stressful travel schedule. He says, "I was suddenly very hungry to see to it that all parts of my life hung together as one integrated whole."

He started the journey to wholeness when he was about three years old. He recalls, "I can remember as a very young child being puzzled about human nature—and perhaps most of all puzzled about my own nature and experience. I had continually sought answers in a variety of ways from my parents and authority figures. My parents were loving and well-meaning people, but they rarely talked to me about the big questions."

From parents and authority figures, Fred turned next to "the god of our modern world—science." He turned away from heart to head and spent a couple of decades searching for meaning through biology and psychology. Eventually, he tired of that struggle and concluded that "the only real security in this life was to have financial independence."

That "dry hole" didn't last as long. Financial success didn't deliver either meaning or independence.

So, he began asking, What's it all about? and listening more deeply—listening to his clients, his friends, his wife, and his children. But most of all, he relates, "I've been listening to my heart, to quiet voices when I meditate, pray, and worship. I've been listening when I walk on our farmland. And I've been quietly led to seek wisdom and answers from the most unlikely places."

Fred became fascinated with and a student of the Amish culture. He claims that the Amish live by specific decision rules. Before the elders will embrace a new invention or accept a change, they must be convinced that the change both enhances and supports family and community life. Further, it must not harm the earth, as the Amish see themselves as stewards of the earth.

Studying and visiting the Amish has helped Fred "peel the layers of the onion to arrive at the heart," or more precisely, at his heart! From this point forward, Fred wants to live in ways similar to the Amish values. He wants his behavior to enhance his and others' family and community life and to have a low impact on the environment.

Living with these values in mind has helped Fred re-shape a lot of his choices. It's no longer enough to just get up in the morning to make money as a psychologist. He states, "I still want to make money, but I now want to work on purpose. I want my professional behavior to meet my values. I want to work with clients who I know are in alignment with my purpose."

Fred's purpose each morning is simply this: "In all relationships I want to be a force to help people with matters of the heart." He believes that when people are grounded and live well from their hearts, they naturally tend to make choices that are good for family life, for community life, and for the environment.

Like the Amish, Fred's calling has a spiritual grounding. As he sums it up, "I want to devote the balance of my life to serving God as I have come to understand the divine." In the second half of the purpose journey, he feels at peace about many of the mysteries of life. He's concluded, "I don't need to understand any more about human nature than I already know, and I guess I don't understand it much more than I did at age three."

Every one of us, simply because we are human, periodically wonders, What's it all about? Most major spiritual traditions—Buddhism, Hinduism, Judaism, Christianity, and Islam—deal with this question. We have to work at finding our authentic self and true calling. If we act from a false self—based on superficial values and outer success—we will always jump from one illusion to another. We will never be deeply fulfilled or happy.

Action: Take a 24-hour retreat (see Chapter 9) to reflect on the What's it all about? question.

Lesson 4: Avoid the Pursuit of Happiness

Researchers at the University of British Columbia, Vancouver, and Harvard Business School wondered if money really could make people happy. They theorized that how people spend their money might make a difference or even be as important as how much money people earn. Led by social psychologist Elizabeth Dunn, the researchers conducted a series of studies.[21]

First, they asked a nationally representative sample of more than 630 Americans to rate their general happiness, report their annual income, and provide a breakdown of their monthly spending, including bills, gifts for themselves, gifts for others, and donations to charity.

"Regardless of how much income each person made," Dunn reports, "those who spent money on others reported greater happiness, while those who spent more on themselves did not."

In another experiment the researchers gave participants ether five or twenty dollars, and asked them to spend the money by 5:00 PM that day. Half the participants were instructed to spend the money on themselves (pay a bill or indulge in a treat), and half were assigned to spend the money on others (donate to charity or give a gift). Participants who spent the money on others reported feeling overwhelmingly happier at the end of the day than those who spent the money on themselves.

A corollary study was conducted with people spending their own money, and the results were consistent. The researchers also found that the amount of money, five or twenty dollars, was inconsequential.

So money can buy happiness—if you spend it on others!

Most of us feel somewhat entitled to happiness, or at least we are curious about it. After all, the U.S. Declaration of Independence clearly states, "We hold these truths to be self-evident, that all [people] are created equal, that they are endowed by their Creator with certain unalienable rights, that among these are life, liberty and the pursuit of happiness."

Perhaps the biggest surprise in the study came when people were invited to predict the outcome of the experiment. Most thought that spending money on themselves would make them happier, but in fact the opposite was true—it is spending on others, particularly on experiences with others, that makes people happy.

Action: Offer a surprise—buy an unexpected experience for someone today. How did it make you feel? Happy?

Happiness Explained

Despite an almost universal belief to the contrary, the pursuit of happiness as it is interpreted today is a myth. Ease, comfort, and a state of having arrived do not constitute happiness for most human beings.

The fact is, satisfaction always leads to dissatisfaction! A life without intention and purpose leads to a sparse and shallow existence. Comfort and leisure are great, but they're just not enough. If this were the case, the large number of us who enjoy relative affluence would be ecstatically happy.

So what is this thing called happiness? People frequently claim to define it, but others conclude that individuals must define happiness for themselves. What's more, happiness is always changing. Or is it? Is happiness fame, power, money? Is it marriage, family, community? Is it self-awareness, mindfulness, enlightenment? Is it doing work you love, painting a picture, or creating something beautiful? Or is it all of the above? And will it be the same tomorrow—will your happiness last?

Happiness is now considered a legitimate subject for academic study as well as research. More than two hundred colleges and universities offer courses in positive psychology with a focus on happiness. Positive psychologist Martin Seligman has proposed that we all have an "emotional baseline—a level of happiness" to which we almost inevitably return.

According to Sonja Lyubomirsky, psychology professor and author of *The How of Happiness,* one's happiness level is determined by three things: fifty percent by one's emotional baseline, ten percent by one's life circumstances, and forty percent by "intentional activity."[22] She coined the phrase "40 percent solution": You can boost your happiness by forty percent if you engage in purposeful activities.

In short, we cannot pursue happiness. It must ensue from choosing to live an intentional and purposeful life. Yet for every person who summons up the energy and courage to ask, "What's my purpose in life?" there are many others who hope that more pursuit will feed their hunger.

Action: Stop for a moment and ask yourself, Why do I get up in the morning? Repeat the question several times out loud. Does your answer satisfy you?

CHAPTER 13

Living with Presence

〜

How we spend our days is, of course, how we spend our lives.
ANNIE DILLARD

Annie Dillard's reflection on presence is intriguing. But, what exactly makes presence possible?

The concept of presence is grounded in the practice of mindfulness—the ability to fully inhabit our daily experience. Mindfulness is an antidote to stress and anxiety. The root of our anxiety is our tendency to live for the future which keeps us from fully inhabiting the present.

Living with presence, of course, through the busy routines of work and life is not easy.

The late aikido master and author, George Leonard, observed, "We are always practicing something." However, we are in great need of mindful practices to stay present. Yet we create little time for regular practice. It is through consistent practice that we see beneath the surface to the place where we know not with the mind, but with the heart. Here our intuitive side recognizes a power beyond the natural and rational, and we are able to accept the unknown on faith.

In my working with clients, I ask them to start over again, to become beginners. In *Zen Mind, Beginner's Mind,* Zen master Shunryu Suzuki Roshi writes, "In the beginner's mind there are many possibilities, but in the expert's there are few."

There are steps we can take to live with purposeful presence. This chapter suggests two practices that will help you stay present: Push the pause button then take regular time alone, or "solos," and start a Purpose Practice Group.

But first, let's look at the costs of not practicing presence.

Simple but Not Easy

Mindfulness is an ancient Buddhist practice that has practical relevance for our daily lives today. The term "mindfulness" is often used by spiritually-minded people to describe important but hard-to-reach mindsets. Christian monks, Hindu sages, and Buddhist ascetics all speak of reaching moments of mindfulness through meditation and other practices.

While it may be simple to practice mindfulness, it's not necessarily easy. It requires effort and discipline.

Unfortunately, the way in which these spiritual people portray mindfulness has a tendency to put a lot of people off. It can all sound too spiritual and touchy-feely. Mindfulness, in fact, can be defined scientifically in rational and secular terms. But, most of all, it has to do with being in touch.

Whenever I bring up the topic of "being mindful" in my workshops or coaching, I usually get the response, "Who has time? I'm too busy!" That is a symptom of the problem. Busyness is crowding out our awareness of what is happening in and to our lives. Our very sense of humanity—our full-bodied presence in our lives—is being hijacked by hurry sickness. Symptoms include always rushing somewhere else, never being conscious of being anywhere; always doing, never contemplating what we are doing and why; and not being clear about why we get up in the morning.

This situation was brought home clearly in a provocative YouTube video, "No Time to Think,"[23] by David Levy, a professor in the Information School at the University of Washington. The video offers a disturbing wake-up call, showing how American society has become enslaved to an ethic of "more-better-faster" and is losing touch with the capacity for reflection and being present.

Levy's research focuses on why the technological devices (such as my iPhone!) that are designed to connect us also seem to powerfully disconnect us. It appears that although our society supposedly prizes creativity and innovative thought, it in fact gives little credence to intuition and contemplative practices. Twitter may be the next level of connection, but surely there is something strange and ironic about the popularity of tweeting as our human moments of present time dwindle.

Instead of connecting us, our communication technologies are isolating us, until isolation has become the norm. E-mail, voicemail, instant messaging, mobile phones, text messaging, Facebook, Twitter, and of course the World Wide Web all serve useful roles. But these tools for connecting also crowd out deeper, face-to-face connections in our relationships and add to the level of busyness we perceive.

According to Thomas Eriksen of the University of Oslo, author of *Tyranny of the Moment,* the digital environment favors "fast-time" activities—those that require instant, urgent responses. Such activities tend to take precedence over and shut out "slow-time" activities, such as reflection, play, and "courageous (deep) conversations."[24] The right-now is trumping the timeless—high tech is hijacking the high-touch practices that we desperately need to be present to others and to ourselves. This is a major loss, and we are becoming overwhelmed and tired in the process.

Neuroscientists speak of a lower part of the brain they term "reptilian mind" and tell us that under its influence, we focus on things that are immediately relevant. However, at rare moments, late at night or early in the morning when our bodies are relaxed and quiet, we are able to tap into a mindful state. In this state— what neuroscientists call our neocortex—is the heart of purpose and compassion. We let go of our daily distractions and, often, connect with a more universal perspective. With mindful presence, our mind moves beyond its self-interests. We start to think of other people in a more meaningful way.

Push the Pause Button

To allow ourselves to be truly in touch with what matters at the moment, we have got to pause in our experience long enough to let the present moment sink in.

An important way to practice presence is to push the pause button. Plan regular times for mindfulness—"solos" during which you can be quiet and not distracted by the usual busyness. Hearing a calling requires listening alone. As we take regular solos, we begin unmasking illusions. Slowly we start discerning what parts of our busyness are expressions of our real priorities.

When we get out of touch with our core, we lose our life perspective. We gain back our energy and focus by mindfulness—by pausing regularly. Pushing the pause button enhances our focus and taps our deep energy.

My good friend and colleague, Kevin Cashman, author of *The Pause Principle,* advises the CEOs and world leaders that he coaches to "pause to perform." Kevin claims that "paradoxically, pause powers purposeful performance." As a lifelong meditator, he has practiced pause for many years and defines it: "The Pause Principle is the conscious, intentional process of stepping back, within ourselves and outside ourselves, to lead forward with greater authenticity, purpose, and contribution."

Sometimes we are receptive to pausing; at other times we are not. When crises drop into our lives, we are forced to pause. At times when things seem to be going smoothly, we may not sense the need at all. Yet our mindfulness contracts silently from lack of use.

Kevin wisely says that, "Pause is an inherent, generative principle that is always available to us. Either we consciously, go to it, integrating it into our lives, or it comes to rescue us."

For many of us, a pause practice may seem strange or difficult, yet a solo can help us recalibrate our priorities. But what is a *solo* and what is *"soloing?"* Soloing is simply a process of sitting quietly, taking three deep breaths, and listening.

"How do I take a solo?" First of all, take three deep breaths! In the morning, for instance, get up a little earlier, and before you get involved in anything, just sit quietly and take three deep breaths. Then focus on your day ahead. Picture yourself moving through an ideal day of purpose moments. Envision how you can grow and give in the day ahead. An architect first has an idea or a plan, then designs a building. An artist often has a similar inspiration. Think of your solo as time to create a blueprint for your day.

Take a solo every day. Some are more inclined to create solo time when they're driving long distances, walking, jogging, listening to music, praying, or meditating.

Ideally, we should not let a day pass without pausing—spending some solo time. Eventually we really start unlocking our purpose. The solo is a practice to help us stay on purpose.

Stopping

The solo is about stopping and being present, that is all. Are you able to come to a stop in your life, even for five minutes? Could it be this moment?

Solitude and relaxation both play important roles in reflection. In a quiet, relaxed state, we find it easier to concentrate our energy in the direction we choose and to develop a clearer perception of the purpose moments in our lives. Try this five-minute stopping exercise:

- Push the pause button. Turn off all your devices.

- Sit in a comfortable position. Consciously examine your physical tension and describe it to yourself in detail. Examine its intensity. Become as aware as you possibly can of any tension and related discomfort.

- Close your eyes. Take three slow, deep breaths, breathing from your abdomen. Breathe in and out through your nose, taking breaths that are long and slow. Silently count "one" as you inhale and "two" as you exhale. Do this over and over again for several minutes.

- After you have enjoyed the quiet for several minutes, spend a couple more minutes picturing your day as ideal, happening just as you want it to. You might want to ask: Why am I getting up this morning? Where do I see the possible purpose moments? How can I grow and give today?

- Keeping the pictures in your mind, affirm silently to yourself, "I will make a difference in one person's life today" Picture who that person might be.

- Don't be in a hurry to open your eyes. Before you do, suggest to yourself that you are living on purpose, today.

As you see, the pause practice is relatively quick and simple. Using it really effectively, however, requires stopping.

If we are sincere in our intention to stay on purpose, we will soon find that the solo experience will become easier and more consistent, and we will look forward to being by ourselves. Try it daily for a week with an open mind and heart, and then judge whether it is useful.

If we continue using and developing the solo habit, the changes in focus and in our energy will become an integral part of our lives and our days. Our awareness will become continuous, a state of mindfulness. The solo is one of the most simple, powerful practices we have at our disposal. Energy follows purpose.

Can you create a pause space in your daily calendar to provide "solo" time?

Start a Purpose Practice Group

Another way to live with presence is to start a Purpose Practice Group to enjoy exploring *The Power of Purpose* and the pleasure of each other's company. The book serves as a catalyst for thoughtful inquiry and staying on purpose, and sometimes people find it easier to begin a process if they can share progress with others.

The Purpose Practice Group is patterned after a group that Benjamin Franklin established in 1727. His group, called the Junto, met every Friday night in a room over a tavern in Philadelphia. Franklin claimed the club was "the best School of Philosophy, Morals and Politics that then existed in the Province." Every meeting opened with a set of "queries" (both pious and practical) with a pause between questions, when one might fill and sip a glass of wine. The Junto endured thirty years; Franklin even thought of making it international.[25]

My annual "Back to the Rhythm" expedition in Tanzania is a "walking purpose practice group." Three weeks on a walking safari in the bush and "off the grid" offers twelve people a rare opportunity to pause and reflect. It takes, on average, three days for people to put away their watches and become fully present with the rhythm of a nature and their own nature as well. Sitting around an acacia campfire each evening opens up the purpose conversation at a deep level.

Most of us don't need (or want) to trek in Africa to "get back to the rhythm." But, we can create our own Purpose Practice Group. To start a group, ask two or more people to join you. Try to enlist people with one or more of the following qualifications: they are interested in exploring the topic of purpose; you feel comfortable talking openly with them; they will agree to meet with you four times; they will read the book and answer selected questions before each meeting; and they feel comfortable with being transparent.

Purpose Practice Group meetings can be held around breakfast or lunch, after work, or any time that people can commit to two hours of rich dialogue.

Participants should complete the specific reading and reflection assignments (see the Purpose Practice Group in the Resources section at the back of the book).

Who might you invite to join you in a Purpose Practice Group? Who do you feel comfortable discussing the big questions with?

CHAPTER 14

Communities With Purpose

Many persons have a wrong idea of what constitutes true happiness. It is not attained through self-gratification, but through fidelity to a worthy purpose.

HELEN KELLER

Fidelity to worthy purposes strengthens communities. We are born as purpose-seeking creatures. Purpose is necessary for our very health and longevity. If you doubt this, check out the rates of illness and death when people lose or give up their sense of purpose. We all know people who retire without something to retire to. They have a much higher incidence of early mortality and illness than do those who have a purpose.

Research is beginning to validate what many people have known intuitively all along: When it comes to healthy communities, purpose is working in our favor. A sense of meaning grows out of the choices that we make together. Meaning develops as we share the purpose moments in life. When we have fidelity to shared purposes in life, we often find a spiritual home, and a greater sense of well-being arises in our day-to-day community interactions.

This chapter will help you see the connection between purpose and community.

The Purpose Project

With the upsurge of interest in the connection between community and health, practitioners of "functional" medicine are researching the relationship between meaning and health and longevity. More and more studies are indicating that when we are connected to something larger than ourselves, we strengthen our ability to cope with life's challenges.

No one knows precisely how purpose affects community. Some experts attribute the positive effect to hope, which has been shown to benefit our immune system. Others point to our social connectedness.

However, a growing body of research and practice suggests that people who feel that their life is part of a larger community have stronger immune systems, lower blood pressure, a lower risk of heart attack and cancer, plus they live longer—seven years on average—than those without such a belief. When we are connected to something larger than ourselves, we also strengthen our capacity to cope with life's challenges and transitions. One result of this research and practice has been an enormous increase in the number of U.S. medical schools that teach courses on spirituality and healing—from three in the mid-1990s to seventy-two of 125 medical schools now.

The University of Minnesota's Center for Spirituality and Healing, which is part of the Academic Health Center, enriches well-being and community connectedness through education, research, and innovative programs that advance functional health and healing. The timing was just right when the center's pioneering founder and director, Mary Jo Kreitzer, invited me to become a senior fellow at the center. Together we would create The Purpose Project to advance the understanding of how purpose was fundamental to well-being, and ultimately, communities.

The project has had an impact since day one. Our purpose—"creating more healthy communities through the power of purpose"—led us to sponsor the Second Annual National Positive Aging Conference, with an emphasis on the role of purpose in aging and community. Through our Purpose outreach workshops, we have offered hundreds of people the time, tools, and framework to create a positive-life plan. Our vision—to create healthy communities—is taking hold through partnerships like The Vitality Project.

The Vitality Project

The Purpose Project teamed up with The Vitality Project and the citizens of Albert Lea, Minnesota,[26] to conduct an experiment to measurably improve the well-being of their entire community. Rather than just promoting diet and exercise messages, the Vitality Project implemented lessons from the "Blue Zones"—the longevity hot spots around the world. Led by National

Geographic global explorer Dan Buettner, who authored the best-selling book *The Blue Zones*,[27] a team of committed public servants and community volunteers implemented an innovative and comprehensive makeover of an entire town.

The Blue Zones Vitality Project implemented the nine "lessons from the people who live the longest," detailed in Buettner's book. The Blue Zones approach was to set up four environments of community life to support healthy choices, including the following criteria: Is the town easy to walk and bike through? Are friends supportive? Are homes and offices set up to make healthy choices easy? Do we wake up with a sense of purpose?

The project's goal was to transform the environments of people's lives to increase longevity by an average of two years per person. National experts (including me) were brought in to teach participants about best practices. Around twenty-five percent of the adult population of the community participated through over a dozen concurrent initiatives implemented during just ten months. Participants took an online Vitality Compass® quiz at the beginning and end of the project. The quiz at the end of the project showed projected longevity increases of 2.9 years!

Cathy and Kevin Purdie attended a workshop on Finding Your Purpose. Cathy was already very committed to improving the town by convincing more than two-thirds of restaurants to offer healthier choices. But in this workshop, these busy working parents uncovered a shared vision to be better role models for their children. They found that this could be done best by finishing their college degrees, which they started working on weeks later. When I visited with the Purdies at the project's completion celebration, they introduced me to their beaming children, who were obviously proud of their parents' decisions to finish their educations. Kevin said, "A clear sense of purpose was the essential tool that got us going, and it is essential for any person striving for a healthy life."

Nearly a thousand people (seven percent of the adult population) attended purpose workshops, resulting in 2,276 volunteer hours logged and the launch of a new volunteer-matching website. The increased "purpose moments" were harder to measure, but the mood of service and community was inspiring. Community is not only a place but also a state of mind, and that mindfulness begins from within. It begins with hope, a sense of what's possible, a commitment to a cause, a yearning to solve a problem, or a restless need to express one's creativity in service to the community.

The project, as planned, created a replicable model that received extensive national media attention. Because of the exceptional coverage, requests for similar projects came from around the country. As the citizens of towns across the country realign internal and external environments, they will find that healthy, purposeful choices become wise choices.

The Reimagine Project

Leaders and citizens, of Edina, Minnesota, are also creating a new city vision—Edina Reimagined.

It started as a series of conversations between Edina Mayor, Jim Hovland, and me. He shared with me: "I get a lot of people who are retired and call asking how they can help the city. They are excited to stay involved."

The conversations evolved into some prototype events where we were encouraged to reach out to citizens of all ages. We discovered that both old and new generations of citizens were looking for experiences that connected them to a community purpose, enabling them to have a social impact and meet like-minded people. We discovered, also, that many organizations in the community were undergoing a fundamental shift from emphasizing just profit to emphasizing social good and employee purpose.

This raised a number of questions: How can Edina prepare for this shift in mindset among its citizens? What qualities would make Edina successful at meeting these wants? How can Edina enable its residents to live lives filled with purpose and meaning? How should we think about a "purposeful community?" Just as a city provides the infrastructure—streets, buildings, schools, power, water, government—necessary for people to live and work, how could Edina provide the foundation for citizens to choose a more meaningful lifestyle for their whole lives?

To begin formulating answers, a coalition of Edina

leaders partnered with AARP's "livable cities" initiative, and with Life Reimagined, LLC, to launch "Edina Reimagined." The first step was to convene a "summit" meeting of over two-hundred citizens—the mayor, policy-makers, school superintendent, business leaders, chamber of commerce, entrepreneurs, activists, and citizens—to launch the project.

Topics of workplace, retirement, volunteerism, lifelong learning, health, and culture found their voices heard. Given a diverse group of thinkers and doers, it can be difficult to develop a common language, a common platform, and singular shared vision for a "purposeful community." But, this was a positive first step.

The launch created a buzz in the community and an initial purpose: "To develop a community-based program that espouses the ideals of purposeful living and assists individuals through life's transitions."

Next, Edina leaders chose a leadership task force to follow-up quickly with a series of "Life Reimagined Checkups." Built around Life Reimagined's six-step methodology, this 120-minute experience helped people understand where they are in life and what their next move could be. These programs, free to the public, engaged people in personal reflection, insightful activities, and meaningful networking. The checkups filled up quickly, signaling a latent interest in the community.

The Edina Reimagined program is still in its infancy. But, the plan is to roll out more first-of-its-kind programs and services that provide online and local/

live programs, tools, content, book clubs, meet-ups, and events to support "purposeful living."

What might a Reimagined Edina look like in the future? We don't have a full picture, but here are five attributes worth working toward:

- A purposeful city has citizens who are actively engaged.

- A purposeful city measures its success in human terms, not solely economic ones.

- A purposeful city provides places and opportunities for meaningful interactions.

- A purposeful city encourages "ageless aging" and healthy lifestyle.

- A purposeful city provides lifelong learning opportunities.

Developing these attributes will be the primary challenge for many cities in the twenty-first century. Perhaps, Edina will be a model reimagined city.

"Helper's High"

We are discovering with the Vitality Project, The Purpose Project, and The Reimagine Project that what most people really want is not just longevity—more years to live—but years that are vital, meaningful, and shared.

Healthy community life extends beyond the physical to include the emotional, social, and spiritual. This is everyone's ultimate goal—more years of shared healthy life. So what is the key to creating healthy, purposeful communities?

Neuroscience and researchers are beginning to understand the benefits of expressing care and compassion. They report that we experience distinct physical sensations while we are helping. Some describe these feelings as a "helper's high." People who experience "helper's high" say they feel lighter and more energetic. Other people experience calmness and compassion.

There is increasing evidence that the physical and emotional sensations experienced by people who are helping others are a result of chemicals in the brain. Chemicals, called endorphins, the body's natural painkillers and mood enhancers, have the capacity to stimulate feelings similar to those reported in "helper's highs." Doing good increases endorphins and other positive chemicals. Self-absorption decreases the production of such chemicals. More research, of course, is certainly required.

People with acute or chronic illness are by no means excluded from experiencing "helper's high." When our way of life is dramatically changed by illness or disability, as it was for Nancy Gunderson, the change not only forces us to reevaluate our lives and let go of previous ways of being but can stimulate a search for new sources of community connection.

Physical illness or disability may take away independence and make inaccessible those things that provided, or might have provided, purpose and meaning when we were healthier and more able. However, one of the great truths of purpose is that it is not limited by circumstances. In fact, major challenges may offer the choice of new directions and purpose that can add years of healthy life. The failure to reimagine purpose and direction in such situations can—and often does—result in depression, despair, and the drain of indecision.

As a young woman, Nancy Gunderson loved the outdoors and wilderness, canoeing as much as the intellectually challenging world of archeological and historical research allowed. Her plans included a career in museum administration, more European travel to use her four languages, to research family genealogy, and to marry and have children.

Nancy's life contracted sharply when she came down with a debilitating illness in her late twenties. As her strength and energy drained and her pain level increased, she first gave up her plans for graduate school and dreams of having a family, then even her career. On full disability, unable to drive, for the last twenty years Nancy has depended on a care network of friends to do what she can no longer do for herself: shop for groceries, clean her condo, do her laundry, drive her to doctor appointments. Once comfortable traveling around Oslo, Frankfurt, and Paris on her own, Nancy is now limited to the hallways of her condo, which she travels in her electric wheelchair, or the occasional outing that friends provide.

Yet Nancy lives a life on purpose. She is an attentive and loving aunt to her three nephews who live three states away. It is beyond her ability to visit them, but she is still involved in their lives via Skype. The friends who shop, clean, and do her laundry always find wise counsel and encouragement, thoughtful gifts, and playful humor at her table over a cup of coffee. She watches out for her frail, elderly condo neighbors, whom she has befriended, and calls their family members when they need help. Still a whiz at leading book group meetings and probing financial reports, she volunteers as treasurer on her condo board, and although the effort leaves her bedridden for several days following each board meeting, she has managed to get budgeting for needed building maintenance on track.

Nancy may lack health, strength, and energy, but she finds a "helper's high" in caring for others as they care for her.

The purpose-filled person in an assisted-living facility, nursing home, or other institutional setting may decide to give the gifts of listening and companionship by initiating conversations with other residents, offering time for listening, and, if needed, providing encouragement and hope. Serving in this way empowers people who are ill and gives them a reason to get up in the morning. As their lives take on new meaning, the body's natural healing mechanisms may be invigorated, and years of healthy life may be added.

We Need Stress

To create healthy lives and healthy communities, we need stress. Yes, you read that correctly. We all know that stress can be negative. In the United States, stress results in absenteeism and medical expenses that cost the economy two hundred billion dollars a year. Stress can even be deadly. Obviously, we need less, not more, of that kind of stress.

What we need is the right amount of the right kind of stress. Not only too-great demands but also the opposite—the lack of purpose—may cause disease.

Many would argue that serving or expressing goodwill toward others provides a needed positive stress. Hans Selye, the medical researcher who coined the term *stress,* has suggested that the way to enjoy a rewarding lifestyle free of disabling stress is to practice "altruistic egoism." In essence, this involves serving others.

Selye points out that our biological nature drives us toward self-preservation, or what might commonly be called selfishness. Selye's line of thought suggests that only by linking this self-centered innate nature with an attitude of earning the goodwill and respect of others through altruistic efforts will a happy, meaningful life result.

We may never fully understand our altruistic urge, let alone human nature, but the heart of a purposeful community is centered in the simple idea of caring for our fellow human beings—and caring for ourselves in the process.

We can choose to make our caring for each other be what our lives are all about. The challenge is for us to discover what kind of caring provides that feeling of community we seek. We are not searching for stress per se but rather are searching in particular for tasks whose completion will add meaning to our lives.

Are you living in a "purposeful community?" Are you getting your "minimum daily requirements" of "helper's high?"

CHAPTER 15

Can Science Explain Purpose?

∽

*Everyone who is seriously involved in the pursuit of
science becomes convinced that some spirit is
manifest in the laws of the universe,
one that is vastly superior to that of man!*

ALBERT EINSTEIN

Is purpose spiritual?

There is more to understanding the human condition than some scientists often will admit. From birth onward, we are all growing older. But, we are also growing up, or maturing spiritually. Aging belongs to the body, and maturing belongs to the spirit. Aging requires nothing special from us; maturing requires a spiritual path. Purpose is spiritual wisdom embodied.

Even Einstein seemed to mature spiritually as well as in years. But unless we make conscious choices to do so, we may simply grow old. Even the term "spiritual" comes loaded with cultural baggage. Using the term becomes immediately suspect for many, scientist or not. Much debate between science and spirit comes from the baggage that weighs on the mindset of both camps. Science and spirituality validate the necessity of one another. A notion that is frustrating, often, for proponents in both camps.

The struggle to blend the spiritual and the scientific has been addressed with varying degrees of sensitivity by some of history's greatest minds.

This chapter will explore the natural links between the spirituality and the science of purpose.

Spiritual Maturity

If we live as victims, without consciousness, we simply grow old. But when we age with conscious choice, we can walk the path of purpose, and we grow whole, mature, and wise. These are the only two choices.

What stands in the way of choosing a spiritual path to purpose? Time. The number one pressure on people today is lack of time. Technology encourages us to be "on" twenty-four hours a day, seven days a week via computers, smart phones, and other devices. Electronic gadgets have done away with boundaries to work, making us available outside normal work hours, even on weekends and holidays and during vacations. For more and more of us, the workday never ends.

We have always had trouble with time. What's different today is that pervasive technology and a mindset that we must respond instantly have accelerated life and made it more superficial. We find it ever harder to be present with ourselves and with others and to connect with a Source larger than ourselves.

As a result, our spirit—in particular, our purpose—suffers. We become purposefully stuck, and a meaningful life falls by the wayside, a victim of our hurry sickness.

"Spiritual but Not Religious"

In the book, *War of Worldviews: Science vs. Spirituality*, the authors, Deepak Chopra and Leonard Mlodinow, argue that there is a war between science and spirituality. Science says spirituality is biased and unscientific. And, spirituality says that science is myopic, exclusive, and unbending. We, the readers, are left to decide how to meld the two worldviews.

People often use the words spirituality and religion interchangeably, but they're not the same. Religion has more to do with following the practices and dictates of a tradition, institution, or community, whereas spirituality is more individual—encompassing our personal experience with a Higher Power. This sentiment is one shared by a quarter of the U.S. population who describe themselves as "spiritual but not religious." This distinction captures part of the debate.

The Spirituality in Healthcare Committee at Mayo Clinic offers the following definition: "Spirituality is a dynamic process by which one discovers inner wisdom and vitality that give meaning and purpose to all life events and relationships."

The committee's report goes on to say that "spirituality as a dynamic process helps individuals discover meaning and purpose in their lives, even in the midst of personal tragedy, crisis, stress, illness, pain, and suffering. This process is an inner quest. This quest involves openness to the promptings of one's soul or spirit, silence, contemplation, meditation, prayer, inner dialogue and/

or discernment. Spirituality empowers a person to be fully engaged in life experiences from birth to death."

To unlock our purpose, we must experience that inner wisdom, through spirituality or religion, which gives meaning and purpose to life.

"Can You Tell Me What My Purpose in Life Is?"

Purpose has little to do with genius or gender, ethnicity or age. It is discovering what we truly care about. It is uncovering the gifts within us and giving them away. It is being thoroughly used up when we die because we gave it all away while we were living.

A young man who was searching for his life's purpose wrote to Rabbi Menachem Mendel Schneerson. He said he had discussed the purpose question with every wise person he had ever come across, had read every book on purpose he could find, and had traveled to faraway places to seek the guidance of some of the greatest spiritual teachers. However, no one had ever been able to tell him what his purpose was. So he asked the rabbi, "Can you tell me what my purpose in life is?"

Rabbi Schneerson responded, "By the time you figure out what your mission is, you will have no time to fulfill it. So just get on with it." In other words, do more acts of goodness, and your life's purpose will unfold before you, one day at a time.

We can spend a lifetime philosophizing about the meaning of life, pondering our place in the universe, and miss out on just getting on with it!

The power of purpose comes from recognizing that we were given another day to live—today—and along with that we were given the choice to make a difference in at least one other person's life. A life of purpose is not self-absorbed soul-searching. It is simply getting on with caring and compassion. Who around us needs a hand? How can we improve the little corner of the planet we live on? What can we do, this very moment, to make a small difference in one person's life?

Unlocking our purpose is, ultimately, a spiritual journey. As we mature, our purpose becomes deeper, richer, and wiser. Purpose begins with the genuine desire to connect with the greatest good within ourselves and others. Charles Handy, in *The Age of Paradox,* wrote: "True fulfillment is, I believe, vicarious. We get our deepest satisfaction from the fulfillment and growth and happiness of others. It takes time, often a lifetime, to realize this. Parents know it well, as do teachers, great managers, and all who care for the downtrodden and unfortunate."

If we are to have livable, sustainable lives in the twenty-first century, purpose and compassion must become our guiding ethos. We each need to strengthen our core capacity for compassion not only to help sustain the world but also to foster our own well-being.

Purpose enhances physical and emotional well-being. A study by psychologist David McClelland found that people who simply watched a film of Mother Teresa providing compassion for the poor in India enjoyed significant positive changes in their immune function.

We can speculate, then, that ignoring the needs of others and focusing entirely on ourselves is likely to have the opposite effect on our immune systems. Whether our purpose, like Mother Teresa, is to serve God, raise healthy children, create a healthier community, or play beautiful music, we are empowered by our purpose.

We may not always see the results our lives have on others, but we can know deep down that we are making some contribution, large or small, to the larger pattern of life. We can know that we make a difference, that our life matters.

The Soul of Purpose

As we work our way toward the purpose of our lives, and find that helping others is more fulfilling than indulging our own wants, we begin to understand that compassion is at the very center of a life lived on purpose. Compassion is the soul of purpose. All major religions and spiritual traditions have understood this and have taught the principle that we are to love and care for our neighbors, in contrast to focusing exclusively on our own needs and wants.

Consider what some of the great wisdom keepers through the ages have taught:

Moses (circa 1400 BC): "Do not seek revenge or bear a grudge against one of your people, but love your neighbor as yourself." *Leviticus 19:18*

Krishna (900 BC): "One who engages in full devotional service, who does not fall down under any circumstances, at once transcends the modes of maternal nature and thus comes to the level of Brahman." *Bhagavad-Gita 14:26*

Gautama Buddha (563–483 BC): "Consider others as yourself." *Dhammapada 10:1*

Confucius (551–479 BC): "He who wishes to secure the good of others has already secured his own."

Jesus of Nazareth (AD 0–32): "Love your neighbor as yourself."

Matthew 19:19: "Do unto others as you would have them do to you." *Luke 6:31*

Muhammad (AD 570–632): "Whatever good ye give, shall be rendered back to you, and ye shall not be dealt with unjustly." *Sura 2:272*

A life centered on compassion is lived for the sake of others. It may be difficult or take what seems like a long time to name our larger purpose, but compassion will keep us on the pathway of discovery.

As our purpose evolves over our lifetime—as it is unlocked—it gives our lives dignity and meaning. We are no longer burdened by compassion and purpose as a sense of duty or moral obligation: We care because it is our reason for being here.

The power of purpose is the power of compassion. It alone is the greatest of all the gifts we have to offer.

"Practice Compassion"

The Dalai Lama wisely said, "If you want others to be happy, practice compassion. If you want to be happy, practice compassion."[28]

Now, neuroscience research confirms that practicing compassion supports not just happiness but brain health and well-being. The Center for Compassion and Altruism Research and Education at Stanford University is researching how compassion—"a natural desire to soothe others' suffering"—shows up in the brain and how it affects our health.[29]

They discovered that compassion ignites a powerful biological response. When practicing compassion we're relaxed, our heart rate and blood pressure decrease, and we're much more open to new ideas. We see the world differently. And the beneficial effect is that we're happier and healthier.

Do Scientists Pray?

The science-spirituality debate is unwinnable. To create a debate between them is self-defeating. Why? Because both science and spirituality can inform purpose with new insight.

Hardly anything illuminates this debate more clearly than Albert Einstein's letter to a young girl. Children have a way of getting down to the essence of things. A young girl named Phyllis posed the question to Einstein in a 1936 letter found in the book *Dear Professor Einstein: Albert Einstein's Letters to and from Children:*

The Riverside Church

January 19, 1936

My dear Dr. Einstein,

We have brought up the question: Do Scientists pray? in our Sunday school class. It began by asking whether we could believe in both science and religion. We are writing to scientists and other important men, to try and have our own question answered.

We will feel greatly honored if you will answer our question: Do scientists pray?, and what do they pray for?

We are in the sixth grade, Miss Ellis's class.

Respectfully yours,

Phyllis

Five days later, Einstein wrote back and his answer speaks to the question we're exploring in this chapter.

January 24, 1936

Dear Phyllis,

I will attempt to reply to your question as simply as I can. Here is my answer:

Scientists believe that every occurrence, including the affairs of human beings, is due to the laws of nature. Therefore, a scientist cannot be inclined to believe that the course of events can be influenced by prayer, that is, by a supernaturally manifested wish.

However, we must concede that our actual knowledge of these forces is imperfect, so that in the end the belief in the existence of a final, ultimate spirit rests on a kind of faith. Such belief remains widespread even with the current achievements in science.

But also, everyone who is seriously involved in the pursuit of science becomes convinced that some spirit is manifest in the laws of the universe, one that is vastly superior to that of man. In this way, the pursuit of science leads to a religious feeling of a special sort, which is surely quite different from the religiosity of someone more naïve.

With cordial greetings,

Yours A. Einstein[30]

The Ultimate Purpose of Life

Now, Einstein was a brilliant physicist, proponent of peace, debater of science and spirituality, champion of compassion, and no stranger to advising people from all walks of life. And, I'm no Einstein, nor am I a scientist; however, if I were to lean toward spiritual thinking or scientific thinking, I'd come out on the spiritual side of the debate. That is where I get a sense of meaning and purpose being integrated with the universe so that it doesn't feel hopeless and meaningless to me.

So, I'd write the following letter to Phyllis:

Dear Phyllis,

I believe that there exists a loving Source that created humans and all beings to fulfill specific purposes in a mysterious and evolving universe.

Our purpose in life is to grow and to give to life through compassionate service to others. Purpose joins self and service into something to live for, a reason to get up in the morning.

Every one of us, including you, Phyllis, is born with unique gifts that are given by that Source. We are called, from cradle-to-grave, to grow and to give those gifts away.

Being human means being free; the essence of our humanness is freedom; the freedom to grow and to give is present in every moment, and in every situation in life.

Death gives instruction to life; the longer we live, the more we grow to understand that compassion is the main lesson that we are here to learn. Compassion is the inner urge we feel to give our gifts to others.

Finally, Phyllis, I believe that the ultimate purpose of life is to die happy; the way to die happy is to be thoroughly used up before we pass on—to be used for the sake of a purpose considered by ourselves as a worthy one.

So, I'm not a scientist, but I pray for compassion in you and me!

Get a Life!

You've heard the phrase: "Get a life." Well, better yet: "Get a purpose in life!" Why?

Dr. Majid Fotuhi, MD, PhD, author of *Boost Your Brain*, reports that "having a purpose in life is one of the most important factors for protecting your brain against cognitive aging. This is because people with a high 'purpose in life score' are 2.5 times more likely to stay sharp in heir seventies and eighties, as compared to those with a low score. In fact according to researchers at Rush University Medical Center in Chicago, the high score individuals cut their risk for developing Alzheimer's disease by half."[31]

But, how could this be possible? Dr. Fotuhi goes on to report "One likely reason is that high score individuals have half as many strokes as the low score group. They also have lower levels of stress hormone, higher levels of of good HDL cholesterol, less inflammation, better sleep, happier mood, and an overall sense of well-being. A recent study from Johns Hopkins University in Baltimore showed that elderly who engaged in a purposeful activity of helping students in public schools for two years improved their cognitive performance and experienced an amazing increase in the volume of brain areas that are critical for memory and learning. This thumb-sized brain area, called hippocampus, shrinks by about 0.5% per year after age fifty. The brain shrinkage was halted in the active group; some were even able to totally reverse the effects of aging in their brain and grow the size of their hippocampus by as much as 1.6%."[32]

The powerful scientific evidence for the biological effects of having a purpose in life has important public health implications. Dr. Fotuhi says, "We need to educate people about the the fact that having a purpose in life can be as effective as any medication they can take to improve their memory and cognitive health. Imagine if there was a drug with evidence for reducing the number of strokes in the brain, lowering your risk of developing Alzheimer's disease, and reversing the effects of aging in your hippocampus. How much would you pay for such a drug? Clearly, there is compelling scientific evidence for the necessity of purpose in our society—now more than ever before!"

Some scientific research now shows clear implications for the benefits of "getting a purpose in life" to health, healing, happiness, and longevity.

Here's one example. Beginning in 1994, Patrick Hill and his research colleagues at Carleton University in Canada surveyed more than six thousand people, aged twenty to seventy years, to assess whether they had a sense of purpose in their lives. He followed them for the next fourteen years. Over the fourteen-year follow-up period, 569 participants (about nine percent) died. Those who died had reported lower purpose in life and fewer positive relations than did the others. Not too surprising.

Surprising, however, was that greater purpose in life predicted lower mortality risk across the entire lifespan, showing the same benefit for younger, midlife, and older participants across the follow-up period. This came as a surprise to researchers. "To show that purpose predicts longer lives for younger and older adults alike is pretty interesting, and underscores the power of the construct," Hill reported.

Hill went on to speculate that, "Our findings point to the fact that finding a direction for life and setting overarching goals for what you want to achieve can help you actually live longer, regardless of when you find your purpose." He further stated, "So the earlier someone comes to a direction for life, the earlier these protective effects may be able to occur."

Previous studies have suggested that finding a purpose in life lowers risk of mortality, above and beyond other factors that are known to predict longevity. But, Hill discovered that almost no research examined whether the benefits of purpose vary over time or after important life transitions.

The researchers are currently exploring whether having a purpose might lead people to adopt healthier lifestyles, thereby extending longevity.

Can Life Purpose Reduce Healthcare Costs?

Recent findings in the journal *Proceedings of the National Academy of Sciences* show that having a purpose in life can motivate individuals to take care of their health—and potentially save large healthcare costs.

The study discovered that those living for a purpose were motivated to live a healthier lifestyle and more likely to utilize preventive health services like cancer screenings. Researchers examined over seven thousand people from the Health and Retirement Study—all of whom were over age fifty, representing a wide range of diverse groups for a period of six years.[33]

People living with purpose were more likely to take advantage of cholesterol checks and colonoscopies, overall. Women with life purposes were more likely to take advantage of mammograms and Pap tests, while men actually spent seventeen percent fewer nights in the hospital.

Researchers are hopeful that further studies of the power of purpose could save enormous healthcare costs.

To that point, AARP's program Experience Corps[34] may have a meaningful solution. For the past decade, the nonprofit has partnered people age fifty-five and beyond with students in kindergarten through third grade who need academic help. Across nineteen U.S. cities, volunteers were doing literacy coaching. And, they are increasing student test scores and well-being.

The unsurprising side effect of the program was that the volunteers also experienced significant well-being improvements, both mental and physical. Their rates of depression fell, and their physical mobility, stamina, and flexibility improved. They also improved in memory.

Medicine can't disregard purpose just because it's not easily measureable. Evidence-based medicine is critical. But, what if doctors wrote prescriptions that helped people develop greater purpose in life?

Prescriptions for Purpose

Could a prescription to develop a sense of purpose in life slow Alzheimer's? We don't know.

But, having a purpose in life has been shown in a recent study to help to protect the brain against the ravages of Alzheimer's. The findings come from Rush University Medical Center in Chicago,[35] where researchers have studied more than 1,500 older adults since 1997. All were free of dementia before the study.

The participants underwent yearly checkups to determine their physical, psychological, and brain health. To measure their sense of purpose, they took a profile answering questions like, "Some people wander aimlessly through life, but I am not one of them."

High scores on the profile of sense of purpose were defined as those who had goals in life and a sense of directedness; felt there is meaning to their present and past life; held beliefs that give life purpose; and had aims and objectives for living.

Low scores lacked a sense of meaning in life; had few goals or aims; lacked a sense of direction; did not see the purpose of their past life; and had no outlook on beliefs that gave life meaning.

In the study, 246 people died, and their brains were studied for signs of plaques and tangles, which build up in the brains of those with Alzheimer's.

The researchers sought to find whether having a strong purpose might bolster the brain, perhaps by strengthening "cognitive reserve"—an enhanced network of interconnections between brain cells that protects against cognitive decline.

They discovered that those who scored high on the sense of purpose survey were just as likely to have plaques and tangles in their brains as those who did not have a strong sense of purpose. But they did tend to score higher on tests of memory and thinking, suggesting the possibility of a strong cognitive reserve.

"These findings suggest that purpose in life protects against harmful effects of plaque and tangles on memory and other thinking abilities," said Patricia A Boyle, PhD, the lead author of the study, which appeared in the *Archives of General Psychiatry.* "This is encouraging and suggests that engaging in meaningful and purposeful activities promotes cognitive health in old age."

While developing a strong sense of purpose is no guarantee that someone will not get Alzheimer's, it may help. The idea of cultivating purpose as a means of improving people's brain health is not implanted in medical practice, but it could be. Still, doctors are not trained (or reimbursed) to coach patients on their purpose in life. But, perhaps, its time has come.

Are Happy People Healthier People?

Researchers who have studied that question on a genetic level report that the answer depends upon our definition of "happiness."

A new study has discovered a strong link between outer eudaimonic happiness and having a vital immune system. Interestingly, having shallower forms of inner hedonic happiness, such as self-gratification, produce the opposite result, weakening the body's immune response.

The research published in the *Proceedings of the National Academy of Sciences,* led by psychologist Barbara

Fredrickson and professor of medicine Steven Cole, measured the activity of key genes that regulate the immune system. Participants revealed their level and type of happiness by answering a series of questions about their well-being.

Not surprisingly, hedonic happiness was associated with higher levels of the sort of immune system genetic activity that is typically ignited by extended periods of stress—activity that can increase inflammation and decrease antiviral responses. In contrast, eudaimonic happiness was associated with lower levels of this unwanted genetic activity. This research suggests that a sense of purpose may have more favorable effects on health than striving toward self-gratification.[36]

Perhaps, our genes are telling us that true happiness requires a genuine sense of purpose greater than and beyond ourselves.

Is Meaning Healthier than Happiness?

Scientific breakthroughs and healthier lifestyles keep pushing life expectancy steadily upward. And, philosophers and scientists continue debating what, ultimately, makes life worth living. Is it a life filled with happiness or a life filled with purpose and meaning? And, is there really a difference between the two?

One luminary weighing in on the question is Nobel Prize-winning Princeton University psychologist, Daniel Kahneman. His claim is that toward the end of life, memories are all you keep. What's in your mind matters more than what you own.[37]

Researchers like Kahneman are exploring the happiness-versus-meaning questions in depth trying to distinguish the differences between a meaningful life and a happy one. Their research suggests there's more to life than happiness. Of course, the debate raises the question, "What does happiness actually mean?" Is it even a question worth debating about?

Roy Baumeister, an esteemed professor of psychology at Florida State University, believes there are differences between a happy life and a meaningful one. He bases that claim on research he published in the *Journal of Positive Psychology,* co-authored with researchers at Stanford and the University of Minnesota.[38]

His research team surveyed 397 adults, searching for correlations between their levels of happiness and meaning. And, not surprisingly, they found that a meaningful life and a happy life often go together—but not always.

Can we live a life of meaning but not happiness? Can we live a life of happiness but not meaning? Now, that's a question for the ages.

Here is what they found. Meaning is not connected with whether one is well, well off, or even feels comfortable in life, while happiness is. More specifically, the researchers identified five major differences between a meaningful life and a happy one:

- Happy people satisfy their wants and needs but that seems largely disconnected from a meaningful life.

- Happiness involves being focused on the present and meaningfulness engages thinking about the past, present, and future.

- Meaningfulness is derived from giving to other people while happiness comes from what they gave you.

- Meaningful lives involve higher stress and challenges.

- Self-expression is important to meaning but not happiness.

In the end, like all good debates, we must come to our own conclusions. But, Baumeister concluded that, "having a meaningful life contributes to being happy and being happy may also contribute to finding life more meaningful." In other words, there's evidence for both.

WARNING!

If we aim strictly for a life of pleasure, we may be on the wrong path to finding happiness. Baumeister echoes the wisdom keepers from earlier in this chapter when he warns, "For centuries traditional wisdom has been that simply seeking pleasure for its own sake doesn't really make you happy in the long run."

To live longer, better, happier, we draw meaning from a larger context. So, we need to look beyond ourselves to find the purpose in what we're doing.

Which brings us back to the earlier wisdom of Viktor Frankl and, specifically, his view on happiness. After experiencing unimaginable human suffering in the Nazi concentration camps, Frankl wrote, "Being human always points, and is directed, to something or someone, other than oneself—be it a meaning to fulfill or another human being to encounter. The more one forgets himself—by giving himself to a cause to serve or another person to love—the more human he is."

Millions of people (including me) have been profoundly moved by Frankl's wisdom. We would agree that the pursuit of meaning is what makes human beings uniquely human. As Frankl claimed, "Happiness cannot be pursued; it must ensue. One must have a reason to be happy."

Is It Worth it?

Are you actively living your values, leaning toward compassion, and getting up in the morning to contribute value to the world?

The purpose quest is filled with questions like this, but I've never heard anyone say "it isn't worth it." People living with purpose tell me how their lives (and their well-being) have been enriched. They tell me about things they have now that they wouldn't have had, and ways they feel now that they wouldn't have felt.

Did the power of purpose solve all their worries and troubles? No. But, they know that they have a different life because of it—a richer, more fulfilling one. And that they're a more alive, vital, and open person because of it. The spirituality and science debate continues.

The power of purpose paves the way for many of us to connect with something greater than ourselves—God, nature, a Higher Power—and to find meaning in our lives. That sense of connection is one of the most powerful forces in health, happiness, and longevity. As you find meaning, you will live longer, better.

Notes

1. For more information about this study, visit www.MatureMarketInstitute.com.
2. O. Carl Simonton, "The Healing Journey" (lecture, Denver, 1996).
3. Terry Fox (1958–1981) was a Canadian humanitarian, athlete, and cancer treatment activist. He is considered one of Canada's greatest heroes—in a public opinion poll he was voted the most famous Canadian of the twentieth century. For more information, see www.terryfox.com.
4. Pat Murphy and William Neill, *By Nature's Design* (San Francisco: Chronicle Books, 1993).
5. Mary Catherine Bateson, *Composing a Life* (New York: Plume, 1990).
6. Peter Drucker, interview, *Psychology Today,* October 1968.
7. Ernest Becker, *The Denial of Death* (New York: Free Press, 1973).
8. Albert Schweitzer, *Peace or Atomic War?* (New York: Henry Holt and Company, 1958).
9. Sigurd F. Olson, *Open Horizons* (New York: Knopf, 1969).
10. The full quotation is "Many people die with their music still in them. Why is this so? Too often it is because they are always getting ready to live. Before they know it, time runs out."
11. Phillip L. Berman, *The Courage of Conviction* (New York: Dodd, Mead, 1985).
12. Richard Gregg, quoted in Duane Elgin, *Voluntary Simplicity: Toward a Way of Life That Is Outwardly Simple, Inwardly Rich,* rev. ed. (New York: Quill, 1998).
13. Howard Gardner, *Multiple Intelligences: New Horizons* (New York: Basic Books, 2006).
14. For more information, visit Inventure—The Purpose Company, www.richardleider.com.
15. Mihalyi Csikszentmihalyi, *Flow: The Psychology of Optimal Experience* (New York: Harper & Row, 1990).
16. Matthew Fox, *The Reinvention of Work: A New Vision of Livelihood for Our Time* (New York: HarperCollins, 1995).
17. Juliet B. Schor, *The Overworked American: The Unexpected Decline of Leisure* (New York: Basic Books, 1991).
18. James A. Autry, *Love and Work: A Manager's Search for Meaning* (New York: Morrow, 1994).
19. Rainer Maria Rilke, *Letters to a Young Poet,* trans. Franz Xaver Kappus, intro. Reginald Snell (New York: Random House, 1984).
20. Deborah C. Stephens, ed., *The Maslow Business Reader* (New York: John Wiley, 2000).

21. Elizabeth W. Dunn, "A Policy of Happiness," UBC Reports 55, no. 1 (January 8, 2009).

22. Sonia Lyubomirsky, *The How of Happiness: A Scientific Approach to Getting the Life You Want* (New York: Penguin, 2008).

23. David M. Levy, "No Time to Think," video of a presentation at Google, www.youtube.com/watch?v=KHGcvj3JiGA.

24. Thomas Hylland Eriksen, *Tyranny of the Moment: Fast and Slow Time in the Information Age* (London: Pluto Press, 2001).

25. Franklin describes the formation of the Junto, also known as the Leather Apron Club, in his autobiography, *The Private Life of the Late Benjamin Franklin*, written in French and first published in English in 1793. I created my own Junto based on Franklin's model.

26. Approximately twenty-three hundred citizens of Albert Lea participated in the Vitality Project from January to October 2009. www.cityofalbertlea.org/doing-business/aarpblue-zones-city-health-makeover/for more information.

27. Dan Buettner, *The Blue Zones: Lessons for Living Longer from the People Who've Lived the Longest* (Washington, DC: National Geographic, 2008).

28. His Holiness The Dalai Lama and Edward C. Cutler, *The Art of Happiness at Work* (New York: Riverhead Books, 2003).

29. For more information visit the Center for Compassion and Altruism Research and Education, www.ccare.stanford.edu.

30. Alice Calaprice, *Dear Professor Einstein: Albert Einstein's Letters to and From Children* (Amherst, New York: Prometheus Books, 2002).

31. From conversations and correspondence with Dr. Majid Fotuhi, Memosyn, Chairman, Neurology Institute, Lutherville, MD, www.memosyn.com.

32. "Having a Sense of Purpose May Add Years to Your Life, Study Finds," May 12, 2014, http://medicalxpress.com/news/2014-05-purpose-years-life.html.

33. For more information visit the Health and Retirement Study, National Academy of Sciences, www.nasonline.org.

34. For more information visit Experience Corps – AARP, www.aarp.org/experience-corps.

35. Rush University Medical Center, Rush Alzheimer's Disease Center, www.rush.edu.

36. For more information visit the National Academy of Sciences, www.nasonline.org.

37. Daniel Kahneman, *Thinking, Fast and Slow* (New York: Farrar, Straus & Giroux, 2011).

38. Roy Baumeister, *Journal of Positive Psychology* (August, 2013).

Resources

∽

The Purpose Practice Group Guide

Session 1: What Is Your Purpose?

Read: The Preface and Part I, Chapters 1–4.

Do: Before the session, answer the following question: If you could live your life over again, what would you do differently? (Preface)
Complete the Purpose Checkup. (Resources)

Discuss: Perform group introductions.
Discuss the Preface question. (Above)
Discuss the purpose checkup. (Above)
Discuss the four "Purpose Myths."

Session 2: The Purpose Quest

Read: Part II, Chapters 5–8.

Do: Review the "Three Stages of Purpose."

Discuss: Discuss "The Three Stages of Purpose." Where do you see yourself? (Chapter 5)
Discuss "What Calls You?" (Chapter 6)
Discuss "What Is Your Gift?" (Chapter 7)
Discuss "What's Worth Doing?" (Chapter 8)
Read aloud the quote by George Bernard Shaw at the beginning of Chapter 8 ("This is the true joy in life...") and discuss it.
Discuss the eight intelligences in Chapter 7.
Compare the top "Gifts" of group members.
Discuss the nine curiosity questions in Chapter 8.
Compare responses to the question, "Curious?" About what?
Ask each member to summarize his or her purpose journey. (about five minutes).

Session 3: Purpose and Work

Read: Part III, Chapters 9–12.

Do: Before the session:

Answer the questions in The 24-Hour Purpose
Retreat. (Chapter 9)

Do the Working-on-Purpose Quiz. (Appendix)

Discuss: Read aloud and discuss each person's purpose
statement.

Discuss the Working on Purpose Quiz. (Appendix)

Session 4: Purpose and Well-Being

Read: Part IV, Chapters 12–15.

Do: Read the section on School-of-Life Purpose Lessons.
(Chapter 12)

Read Chapter 15, "Can Science Explain Purpose?"

Discuss: Discuss the five School-of-Life Purpose Lessons.
(Chapter 12)

Discuss the concept of "Science vs. Spirituality."

Answer the question, "How can I find meaning. Live
longer, better?"

Celebrate!

The Purpose Checkup

Please read each statement carefully and take a few moments to decide on a true response for yourself. Then write the number that most nearly reflects that response. The answers offer the following range of responses:

0. Can't Decide.
1. Definitely disagree.
2. Somewhat disagree.
3. Somewhat agree.
4. Definitely agree.

Having (Outer Life)

_____ I wake up energized about the day ahead.

_____ I feel good about my life and grateful for what I have.

_____ I have taken risks to do things I care about.

_____ I have found ways to offer my gifts and talents to the world.

_____ I'm excited and hopeful about the future.

_____ I don't have many regrets about things I haven't done.

_____ I go to sleep at night feeling that my day was well-lived.

_____ *Total Having Score*

Doing (Inner Life)

_____ Doing things for others is important to me and I make time for it.

_____ When I have key decisions to make, I focus on what deeply matters to me and let that be my guide.

_____ I enjoy being alone.

_____ I know what I'm good at and I use my gifts to make a difference in people's lives.

_____ I have the courage to face my adversities.

_____ I'm growing and giving.

_____ I maintain a balance of saving and savoring the world.

_____ *Total Doing Score*

Being (Spiritual Life)

_____ I sense the presence of a Higher Power.

_____ I maintain a consistent spiritual practice.

_____ I feel a sense of the sacred when I'm in the natural world.

_____ I offer compassion to others readily.

_____ I offer forgiveness to others easily.

_____ I feel a deep sense of gratitude for my life.

_____ I know what I'd like to be remembered for.

_____ *Total Being Score*

_____ **Total Purpose Checkup score**

Interpretation

Having (Outer Life) The dimension of your external experience and activity—how effectively you relate to the "having" choices in your life.

Doing (Inner Life) The dimension of your internal experience and inner activity—how effectively you relate to the "doing" choices in your life.

Being (Spiritual Life) The dimension of your invisible experience and spiritual activity—how effectively you relate to the "being" choices in your life.

Scoring

Your score in each section is one measure of your development in that dimension. Your total Purpose Checkup score (out of 84) gives a measure of the power of purpose you are experiencing in your life at present.

64–84   Yes, living purposefully! You're clear about what truly matters to you and you're mattering in the world.

43–63   Yes, basically fulfilled! Keep on growing and giving in your life.

22–42   Unlocking purpose requires more clarity. The next step: Clarify your gifts, passions, and values.

21–0   Living purposefully isn't reserved for the elite few. So, don't give up because your score right now is low. The power of purpose process works, if you work the process!

The Working-on-Purpose Quiz

Check yes or no according to how you feel about each question today.

Yes	No	
____	____	Do I wake up most Mondays feeling energized to go to work?
____	____	Do I have deep energy—feel a personal calling—for my work?
____	____	Am I clear about how I measure my success as a person?
____	____	Do I use my gifts to add real value to people's lives?
____	____	Do I work with people who honor the values I value?
____	____	Can I speak my truth in my work?
____	____	Am I experiencing true joy in my work?
____	____	Am I making a living doing what I most love to do?
____	____	Can I speak my purpose in one clear sentence?
____	____	Do I go to sleep most nights feeling this was a well-lived day?

The total number of *yes* responses on the inventory provides a general idea of your power of purpose at work. If you have many *yeses,* you're obviously intent on making a difference through your work. You probably have a sense of purpose or direction, but you might consider further clarifying your gifts, passions, and values.

Resources for Reflection

Baumeister, R. F. and Tierney, J. *Willpower: Recovering the Greatest Human Strength.* NY: Penguin Press, 2011.

Berger, Warren. *A More Beautiful Question: The Power of Inquiry to Spark Breakthrough Ideas.* NY: Bloomsbury, 2014.

Bolles, Richard. *How to Find Your Mission in Life.* Berkeley, CA: Ten Speed Press, 1991.

Buettner, Dan. *Thrive: Finding Happiness the Blue Zones Way.* Washington, DC: National Geographic Society, 2010.

Cashman, Kevin. *The Pause Principle: Step Back to Lead Forward.* San Francisco: Berrett-Koehler, 2012.

Christensen, Clayton. *How Will You Measure Your Life?* Harper-Business, 2012.

Crum, Thomas. *Three Deep Breaths: Finding Power and Purpose in a Stressed-out World.* San Francisco: Berrett-Koehler, 2009.

Csikszentmihalyi, Mihaly. *Flow: The Psychology of Optimal Experience.* HarperPerennial, 1991.

Fotuhi, Majid. *Boost Your brian: The New Art & Science Behind Enhanced Brain Performance.* NY: HarperOne, 2013.

Frankl, Viktor. *Man's Search for Meaning.* NY: Pocket Books, 1977.

Grant, Adam. *Give and Take: Why Helping Others Drives our Success.* Penguin, 2014.

Hurst, Aaron. *The Purpose Economy: How Your Desire for Impact, Personal Growth, and Community is Changing the World.* Boise, ID: Elevate, 2014.

Klein, Daniel M. *Travels with Epicurus: A Journey to a Greek Island in Search of a Fulfilled Life.* Penguin, 2012.

Leider, Richard J., and Shapiro, David A. *Claiming Your Place at the Fire: Living the Second Half of Your Life on Purpose.* San Francisco: Berrett-Koehler, 2004.

Leider, Richard J., and Shapiro, David A. *Repacking Your Bags: Lighten Your Load for the Rest of Your Life.* San Francisco: Berrett-Koehler, 2012.

Leider, Richard J., and Shapiro, David A. *Something to Live For: Finding Your Way in the Second Half of Life.* San Francisco: Berrett-Koehler, 2008.

Leider, Richard J., and Shapiro, David A. *Work Reimagined: Unlocking Your Purpose.* Oakland: Berrett-Koehler, 2015.

Leider, Richard J., and Webber, Alan M. *Life Reimagined: Discovering Your New Life Possibilities.* San Francisco: Berrett-Koehler, 2013.

Lyubomirsky, Sonja. *The Myths of Happiness: What Should Make You Happy, But Doesn't. What Shouldn't Make You Happy But Does.* Penguin, 2013.

Palmer, Parker. *Let Your Life Speak: Listening for the Voice of Vocation.* San Francisco: Jossey-Bass, 2000.

Santorelli, Saki. *Heal Thy Self: Lessons on Mindfulness in Medicine.* NY: Harmony, 2000.

Seligman, Martin E. P. *Flourish: A Visionary New Understanding of Happiness and Well-Being.* NY: Atria Books, 2012.

The Purpose Company

↪

Reading a book can be very helpful on the pathway to purpose, and I hope that this book has been useful to you in pursuing yours.

You can travel the purpose pathway further with programs offered by Inventure—The Purpose Company, of which I am founder. We are a firm devoted to helping people unlock the power of purpose.

We offer keynote speeches and seminars for conferences and meetings. We also offer an Inventure Expedition walking safari in Tanzania, East Africa. For more information, go to www.richardleider.com.

In this book, I have shared what I have learned from many wise teachers and readers. I invite you to participate in an ongoing purpose movement. If anything in this book touched you, troubled you, or inspired you, please email me. I am interested in hearing about sources, resources, and stories of people living and working "on purpose." I'll respond. (www.richardleider.com)

Acknowledgments

Many people have helped me along my purpose path. Some have become stories in the text; for this, I offer my gratitude. I also wish to thank all the wise elders and spiritual teachers who have guided me in matters of purpose.

I wish to express heartfelt thanks for the energy and encouragement on this project by my purposeful editor, Neal Mallet, and the truly on-purpose team at Berrett-Koehler, who support the movement toward a more enlightened world of meaning. They are an author's dream team.

Viktor Frankl had a huge influence on my life, career, and writing, and he influenced my whole point of view on purpose. For this inspiration, I am deeply grateful.

And finally, love and gratitude to my wife, Sally. In our relationship I continue to learn about the true power of a purposeful relationship.

Index

~~

About the Author

Richard Leider, founder of Inventure—The Purpose Company, is one of America's preeminent executive coaches. He is ranked by *Forbes* as one of the "Top 5" most respected executive coaches, and by the Conference Board as a "legend in coaching."

Richard's nine books, including three best sellers, have sold over one million copies and have been translated into twenty languages. *Repacking Your Bags* and *The Power of Purpose* are considered classics in the personal development field.

As co-author of *Life Reimagined,* he is the Chief Curator of content for AARP's Life Reimagined Institute. Widely viewed as a visionary and thought leader on the "power of purpose," his work is featured regularly in many media sources including PBS public television and NPR public radio.

As a keynote speaker, he is one of a select few advisors and coaches who have been asked to work with over one hundred thousand leaders from over one hundred organizations including AARP, Ericsson, Mayo

Clinic, MetLife, National Football League (NFL), and United Health Group.

Richard holds a master's degree in counseling and is a National Certified Counselor (NCC), a National Certified Career Counselor (NCCC), and a National Certified Master Career Counselor (MCC). As a Senior Fellow at the University of Minnesota's Center for Spirituality and Healing, he founded The Purpose Project. He is a Carlson Executive Fellow at the University of Minnesota School of Management and co-chairman of the Linkage/Global Institute for Leadership Development.

He is a contributing author to many coaching books, including: *Coaching for Leadership, The Art and Practice of Leadership Coaching, Executive Coaching for Results, The Leader of the Future,* and *The Organization of the Future.*

Richard's work has been recognized with awards from the Bush Foundation, from which he was awarded a Bush Fellowship, and the Fielding Institute's Outstanding Scholar for Creative Longevity and Wisdom Award. He was named a Distinguished Alumni by Gustavus Adolphus College, and to the Hall of Fame at Central High School.

For thirty years, Richard has led Inventure Expedition walking safaris in Tanzania, East Africa, where he co-founded and is a board member of the Dorobo Fund for Tanzania. He and his wife, Sally, live on the St. Croix River outside of Minneapolis, Minnesota.

Also by Richard J. Leider, with David A. Shapiro

Repacking Your Bags
Lighten Your Load for the Good Life, Third Edition

"Living in the place you belong, with the people you love, doing the right work, on purpose." This is how Richard Leider and David Shapiro define "the good life." In this wise and practical guide, Leider and Shapiro help you weigh all that you're carrying, leverage what helps you live well, and let go of those burdens that merely weigh you down. This third edition has been thoroughly revised with new stories and practices to help you repack your four critical "bags" (place, relationship, work, and purpose); identify your gifts, passions, and values; and lighten your load, no matter where you are on your life journey.

"Whether you're starting out on your journey or are well along the way, this classic book will give you the knowledge, insight, and inspiration you'll need for the trip."
—**Daniel H. Pink, author of *Drive* and *A Whole New Mind***

Paperback, 232 pages, ISBN 978-1-60994-549-7
PDF ebook, ISBN 978-1-60994-552-7

BK Berrett–Koehler Publishers, Inc.
www.bkconnection.com   **800.929.2929**

Work Reimagined
Uncover Your Calling

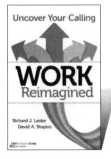

It's vital that we know how to find work that allows us to remain true to our deepest gifts, passions, and values—in short, our "calling." Through using dozens of inspiring personal stories, as well as a unique Calling Card exercise that features a guided exploration of fifty-two "natural preferences" (such as Advancing Ideas, Doing the Numbers, and Building Relationships), Leider and Shapiro give us a new way to uncover our calling.

Paperback, 192 pages, ISBN 978-1-62656-558-6
PDF ebook, ISBN 978-1-62656-559-3

With Alan M. Webber
Life Reimagined
Discovering Your New Life Possibilities

Are you at a point in your life where you're asking, "What's next?" Many of us face these transitions at midlife, but they can happen at any point. Here is your guidance system to help you navigate this new life phase. You can use the powerful practices and insights—enhanced with online tools and exercises at AARP's LifeReimagined.org website—to help you uncover your own special gifts, connect with people who can support you, and explore real possibilities.

Paperback, 192 pages, ISBN 978-1-60994-932-7
PDF ebook, ISBN 978-1-60994-953-2

BK Berrett–Koehler Publishers, Inc.
www.bkconnection.com

800.929.2929

Do You Want to Put Your Purpose to Work?

When you can find work that reflects your deepest values and allows you to express your special gifts, you have found your calling! Everyone has one, and now you can find yours. Richard Leider's Calling Card process starts with cards that identify fifty-two natural "gifts" (such as Writing Things, Creating Dialogue, Seeing Possibilities, Fixing Things). A set of simple instructions walks you through a self-guided exercise that will help you discover the work you were meant to do. Find your real work possibilities today!

ISBN 978-1-62656-701-6. Available online from Berrett-Koehler at www.bkconnection.com/callingcards or from your favorite retailer.

BK Berrett–Koehler Publishers, Inc.
www.bkconnection.com   **800.929.2929**

Berrett–Koehler Publishers

Berrett-Koehler is an independent publisher dedicated to an ambitious mission: *connecting people and ideas to create a world that works for all*.

We believe that to truly create a better world, action is needed at all levels—individual, organizational, and societal. At the individual level, our publications help people align their lives with their values and with their aspirations for a better world. At the organizational level, our publications promote progressive leadership and management practices, socially responsible approaches to business, and humane and effective organizations. At the societal level, our publications advance social and economic justice, shared prosperity, sustainability, and new solutions to national and global issues.

A major theme of our publications is "Opening Up New Space." Berrett-Koehler titles challenge conventional thinking, introduce new ideas, and foster positive change. Their common quest is changing the underlying beliefs, mindsets, institutions, and structures that keep generating the same cycles of problems, no matter who our leaders are or what improvement programs we adopt.

We strive to practice what we preach—to operate our publishing company in line with the ideas in our books. At the core of our approach is stewardship, which we define as a deep sense of responsibility to administer the company for the benefit of all of our "stakeholder" groups: authors, customers, employees, investors, service providers, and the communities and environment around us.

We are grateful to the thousands of readers, authors, and other friends of the company who consider themselves to be part of the "BK Community." We hope that you, too, will join us in our mission.

A BK Life Book

This book is part of our BK Life series. BK Life books change people's lives. They help individuals improve their lives in ways that are beneficial for the families, organizations, communities, nations, and world in which they live and work. To find out more, visit **www.bk-life.com**.

Berrett–Koehler
Publishers

Connecting people and ideas
to create a world that works for all

Dear Reader,

Thank you for picking up this book and joining our worldwide community of Berrett-Koehler readers. We share ideas that bring positive change into people's lives, organizations, and society.

To welcome you, we'd like to offer you a free e-book. You can pick from among twelve of our bestselling books by entering the promotional code **BKP92E** here: http://www.bkconnection.com/welcome.

When you claim your free e-book, we'll also send you a copy of our e-newsletter, the *BK Communiqué*. Although you're free to unsubscribe, there are many benefits to sticking around. In every issue of our newsletter you'll find

- A free e-book
- Tips from famous authors
- Discounts on spotlight titles
- Hilarious insider publishing news
- A chance to win a prize for answering a riddle

Best of all, our readers tell us, "Your newsletter is the only one I actually read." So claim your gift today, and please stay in touch!

Sincerely,

Charlotte Ashlock
Steward of the BK Website

Questions? Comments? Contact me at bkcommunity@bkpub.com.